THE SPIRIT OF THE GREEN MAN

The Spirit of the Green Man

Mary Neasham

Green Magic

This edition is published by
Green Magic
The Long Barn
Sutton Mallet
Somerset
TA7 9AR

Typeset by Academic + Technical, Bristol
Printed and bound by Antony Rowe Ltd.

Cover image by Jane Brideson

Cover design by Chris Render

Cover production by Tania Lambert

ISBN 0 9542 9637 0

GREEN MAGIC

Contents

Acknowledgements

Love, hello and thanks to: My mother Valerie, daughter Gemma and her partner Andy, my brothers Graham and Gavin and partners Charity and Di, my nephews Skye and Joachim and niece Aveline, Pete Gotto for sharing your vision and Chris Render for intelligent deciphering at Green Magic, Jane Brideson for her beautiful artwork, Glennie Kindred and Nick Mann for kind support and input, Royston Baldock and Anna De Benzelle for their friendship and contributions, David Pollard for out of the dark comes your light, Natalie and everyone at Sagecat Moot for your support and friendship, Christina and David, Jessica and David thanks for the trust, Pete Fordham for a lifetime commitment of love to Bradfield Woods, Otter for his wisdom and free spirit, Jill and Brian Claxton (keep up the great work!), Dolores, Carmen would be proud of you, Avril, Toast and Sophie, Louise for her Hindu perspective and wonderful Reiki, to John Clare my favourite nature poet, to all eco-activists and Green campaigners globally, and David Blaine for being in the right place at the right time!

'What if God was one of us?' (Maria Wilson)

And finally to every child of nature who beats true to the drum of life!

About the Author

Mary Neasham is my pen name. I am a forty-one year old single mum living in Suffolk, England. I was born in London and spent most of my younger years living in and near the metropolis. My married years were spent in the beautiful west country that still holds a special place in my heart. Although a child of nature I didn't wake up spiritually until I was about thirty-three. Since meeting a group of pagans from Ipswich in 1999 I realised there were others who spoke my language and I haven't looked back since.

I don't really tread any specific pagan path, preferring instead to tread my own, but I have drawn from many traditional practices over the past few years. I have been labelled mad, Wiccan, Druid, Celtic, Norse to name but a few but it makes no difference to me. I've studied the art of Tarot and Runes but wouldn't consider myself a master of either and always have something new to learn from these crafts.

My real passions are being in nature and exploring my own creativity, but sharing this with others always provides further inspiration that I value deeply.

This book sets out to introduce people to the magic and wonder that is life, especially our ancient mysteries, through communication with the Green Man in your natural environment.

Green Magic entered my life by a chance coincidence and have supported my writing career ever since producing *Teenage Witch's Book of Shadows*, a fun introduction designed for younger people with a serious undertone emphasising self belief, and *Handfasting: A Practical Guide*, exploring the world of marriage, soul binding and guiding others in how they can celebrate their own unions in a magical way.

I have not set out to discredit anyone's beliefs but I do like to challenge perceptions, mine and those of others.

Open your heart and the rest will follow!

Mary Neasham 2003

Introduction

Like many of you now reading this book, my own personal journey with the spirit now universally recognised as 'the Green Man' probably started before I could talk and was most definitely before any conscience awareness of the Green Man as such.

Some of my earliest memories are of looking up to see the distant branches of trees looming over me playing in the breeze, ecstatically invigorating my senses as I waved my chubby arms back at them.

MY PRAM DAYS

Once I'd discovered independent mobility I headed with true and honest intent towards this Great Spirit with every movement I could muster.

Occasionally my attempts at riding the increasing gauntlet of obstacles designed to restrain me from reaching my goal would succeed and I'd reach the front garden to touch upon a spider or hedge, or the laburnum tree whose pods my father warned us were poisonous. Achieving this goal filled me with energy and delight as I briefly interacted with its light and its dark.

MY CRAWLING AND TODDLING DAYS

Our garden blossomed with a veritable buzz of vigour helped on its way by the loving care and attention my parents lavished on it.

I helped to water roses and learnt how to pull up weeds and dispose of them on our compost heap, but it was the little things that I focused on at this time, especially the insect life, and I can remember spending what could often feel like eternity just watching a garden spider in its web or a snail make its way across the path. I'm sure for many of you reading this so far these experiences will reverberate with your own childhood.

Ours was a garden of surprises with the odd clump of asparagus and rhubarb nestled inconspicuously amongst the more traditional suburban blooms of bedding flowers. Each season held new promise and as the early spring bulbs of crocus and snowdrops fell back a sudden burst of yellow daffodils would leap up to take their place. These in turn were followed by clumps of lobelia and the usual bedding plants of late spring but it was always the roses with their magical perfume that I waited for and helped nurse through the growing season.

Autumn would arrive with its own special beauty and colourful tones and all the local neighbourhood children had fun in the leaves and played conkers. As winter set in I especially looked forward to the first frosts to transform the garden into a purified world of crystal. Like all youngsters we prayed for snow and ice so we could build our snowmen and skate on the local pond, something we were only allowed to do if the local park warden accompanied us. Our parents worked on the theory that if the ice could take his weight we would be fine; how times have changed.

The maple tree at the end of our humble patch held court over our horticultural expedience throughout the year as if to say, 'Yeah not bad', or 'OK, but that corner looks dead to me'. We responded to its demands and it gave us beauty and love in return.

In this small and generally insignificant place my connection with natures cycles was initiated. Like many children of my generation I attended Sunday school, my initial agenda was to gain literal Brownie points, but felt that although Christ offered me a humanitarian spiritualism there was 'something lacking'. When we spoke of 'our father' my instinct was to shout, 'But what about our mother too!' but I didn't.

At the end of service I would play the national anthem encouraged by our elderly neighbour who played the church organ. The parishioners tolerated this in quiet bemusement of my feeble musical ability. I don't know what they made of this strange gangly girl turning their attention to our monarch but it was my way of saying, 'we can hold female power in adoration too you know'.

MY FORMATIVE YEARS

Although the garden offered us a sacred family space the local park (a satellite of Epping Forest) had more to offer and called me by day and by night. But unlike the essentially protective environment of the garden this energy felt raw and wild, untameable and deeply seductive.

There was a forbidden element to it, conceived by the general parental fear of local perverts who to this day feel the need to display themselves sexually to unsuspecting young people who wander alone. The park had an even more sinister side to it and sadly a few serious assaults have taken place over the years.

But, undeterred, most of the local children would still venture in during daylight in small groups and explore its varied landscape of woodland and lakes, appreciating its magical omnipresence and, I believe, protected by our friend the Green Man.

We visited it many times as a family, as did most of the local residents, and even to a young child the love and respect our elders felt for this place was obvious. They spoke passionately of their reluctance at any change or externally enforced order over its management and would object instantly if feeling threatened by such actions.

This respect of the essence of our wider sacred space was evident, but was by no means the highest priority.

Like many of my peer group our childhood was bisected at every turn by consumerism and conspicuous consumption. This was the sixties, a gaudy plastic space age of increasing market forces and Keynesian economics. As time wore on my parents and their peers grew drunk with their riches and newly acquired status in the community whilst I partly withdrew into my world of nature and its powerful forces.

As my relationship with the Green Man developed, a global picture began to emerge in my mind and my dreams. It wasn't a pretty one. In reaction I began to speak out and it wasn't always well received. I can remember, for example, embarrassing my mother and father as they bought veal from our local butcher and not being thanked for my shared enlightenment. Occasionally one of my schemes would touch their hearts and I felt closer to them as a consequence. I remember at the age of eight, the age I felt was my favourite one, selling off my entire collection of Teddy Bear comics in aid of banning live exports. I was right about that age though it was possibly the best.

Sadly we all became partly detached from one another and as we increased our material wealth we decreased our integral security as a family unit.

The stresses our modern life put upon my parents was evident to me and I began looking for 'another way'. Like many of my generation I was inspired by dreams of living 'the good life' and strove to achieve something like it rather than being tempted by the lures of the big city and its well-paid jobs. So I opted for a caravan in Epping Forest and years of mucking out and riding horses instead. Whilst my old school friends earned their megabucks and indulged their desires for material possession I survived on a paltry twenty five pounds a week and had some of the happiest years of my life. Being footloose and fancy free in Epping Forest was a great privilege that I will always be thankful for. Being able to get up just before dawn and ride out in the crisp winter frost was and still is like entering the land of pure faerie. This huge ancient forest is one of our best-protected natural environments and is full to the brim with mature oaks, beech, birch and holly amongst many others too numerous to mention. Later on in my life I worked for a mapping project working on a new path finder and was lucky enough to spend a whole month on Amesbury Banks, an ancient iron age camp thought to have been used by Boudicca on her way to London. This place is reputed to be haunted and we all had strange and mysterious experiences whilst being there. One or two people couldn't cope with its energy at all. I enjoyed it, but the mosquitoes can be a real nuisance in June.

I know for a fact that although the spirit of the Green Man has over the years kept me sane, lifted my spirits, fed me, nourished me and occasionally terrified me, I will always have something new to experience and learn from it.

In writing this book I hope to share with you, the reader, the Spirit of the Green Man and prove that he is very much alive and kicking in our fair land today.

The Green Man is my mother, my father, my brothers and my sisters, he fulfils every human and non–human element my soul requires. If I am sad he makes me laugh, if happy he keeps me there, if hurt he allows me to cry, if needy he manifests my desires, if lost he shows me the way even if I don't like the look of the path ahead.

The Green Man can never truly be expressed as a muse for a book but I hope that by sharing some of my lessons and experiences with him I can shed a little light on his manifestation today.

How do I receive your message?
Ask the oak tree.
How will I understand this message?
Listen to the wind.
How will I convey this message?
Watch the leaves.
How will I know if I've succeeded?
See where they fall.

1

The Origins

For some of you reading this book the image of the Green Man is well
known, for others less so. The origins of these carvings and images found
in churches and cathedrals all over Britain and Europe have been steeped
in obscurity. These 'tree faces' come in a huge assortment of styles and
mainly portray male features, although you can come across the odd
female one too. They usually consist of a human face emerging from a
sea of greenery with leaves often sprouting forth from mouths, noses and
ears. The expressions vary considerably from joyous to fierce and every
emotion in between. The obvious conclusion is that the craftsmen who
carved them, and the country people who looked at them, had met the
Green Man in person and knew exactly what he looked like.

Carved beautifully out of stone and wood, they often occupy the
highest elevation in the buildings they reside in. Some excellent British
examples can be found in places such as Canterbury Cathedral in Kent,
Fountains Abbey in Yorkshire, Roslyn Chapel in Edinburgh (which
boasts 103, no less), Wells Cathedral in Somerset, Dorchester Abbey in
Oxfordshire, Hereford Cathedral in Herefordshire, Ely Cathedral in
Cambridge, Norwich Cathedral in Norfolk, and a particularly lovely
multi-seasonal face in All Saints at Sutton Benger in Wiltshire, among
many others far too numerous to mention. The image is also found in
India, the Middle East and the Far East.

Several books are included in suggested Further Reading on page
183 that include more in-depth examinations of these carvings than I
intend replicating.

Finding the origin of his name, 'the Green Man', is simple to prove
as the first two people who made a concerted effort to define him were
the late Kathleen Basford who went on to write the first ever book on the
subject and, coincidentally at around the same time, Lady Raglan in 1939.
[It is, I feel, interesting to note that this was also the year we joined in with
the war against Nazi Germany.] They were equally intrigued and

surprised at the number of 'tree faces' that adorned many a church and other ecclesiastical building all over Europe. Many of the suppositions they drew ranged from the artistic free expression of stonemasons to local folklore and customs.

Once Lady Raglan started investigating our native folklore she began to find evidence in plenty of northern European traditions. The seasonal customs that interested her the most were the May Day celebrations that are, in many towns and villages, still practised to this day.

Most of them include the dressing of young men in leaves and, in some cases, antlers escorting the May queen through the streets to the May pole for the fertility celebrations. Over the past two thousand years of Christianity, in many places, we have held on to this overtly sexual custom from our pagan past throughout the British Isles.

This concept in itself is surprising as one would think it might have been the first to be driven out, once the new moral dictates of Catholicism took hold. Some places, it seems, were more suppressed than others, and it is not surprising to find the traditional practices of May celebrated almost continually in the more rural outlying areas. There was also a revival of many of these old customs around the time of the industrial revolution as we moved toward the new technological age we inhabit today. This time of scientific exploration and widening acceptance of man's desire to understand his environment through intellectual means challenged the preconceived ideals of religion, with Darwin being perhaps the most radical exponent.

One of our most unusual modern examples of the image of the Green Man can be found, surprisingly, adorning the entrance to the Custard Factory arts complex in Birmingham. This mammoth piece appears to have been constructed from stone and vegetation and his face bears an uncanny resemblance to Cernunnos or the Horned God. He is a true giant with an arresting presence and is well worth visiting if you get the chance.

The May Day fertility customs go back to our Bronze Age past and in some cases their roots are even older. Padstow, in north Cornwall, has its annual 'hobby horse' celebration which kicks off on the night of 31 April. Revellers go about the town singing a traditional song and encouraging residents to join in. The following morning the old hoss is brought out from its home at the Golden Lion Inn and is worn as a costume whilst its 'teaser' accompanies it with a club. The 'old hoss' is a mythical mare and its 'teaser', I presume, represents the 'teasing stallion' that is often used to discover whether a mare is in season when taken to stud. During its journey through the town a song is sung and the horse symbolically dies and is re-born by attention from the 'teaser' several times. Further down the Cornwall coast we find Helston and its annual Furry Dance. Otherwise known as the floral dance, it is held on 8 May each year unless that coincides with a Sunday or Monday. Men and women don traditional costume with children dressed in white and wind their way through customary paths even if this means traversing someone's garden or property. There are five dances in all throughout the day with the principal dance being held at midday. The whole town is decorated with early spring bluebells and hazel. The tradition is believed to stem from an old pagan festival of welcoming the spring and bidding the winter a final farewell. It is typical of many throughout Europe and the British Isles. Another typical example is the Garland King celebration at the head of Hope Valley in Castleton, Derby. At two o'clock in the afternoon the people gather to 'dress' the frame that will become the garland. This huge beehive-shaped cone will, once covered in mayflowers, adorn the 'king of summer' whilst the horse he sits upon is led through the streets by his 'queen'. Unable to move, with only his legs visible, his journey completed, he is taken to the church tower. A rope is thrown down by bell ringers who attach the end to the garland and lift it up off the 'king' and raise it on to a waiting pike at the top of the tower. This symbolic decapitation of the old 'king' makes way for the new 'king' of the season and represents as usual the eternal cycle of life and sacrifice or death.

An excellent example of British traditional Jack-in-the-Green celebrations takes place on Bluebell Hill in Kent each May Day morning at dawn. A 'figure' created from branches and ivy about seven feet tall is eventually 'freed' after much merrymaking and the resultant greenery is taken to nearby woods to rot down naturally as in keeping with natures cycle. This annual 'act' is observed by up to a thousand onlookers, all keen to be a part of this ancient custom.

One of the most durable and indeed unique practices rooted in the Green Man tradition we have in this country is morris dancing. All over the country there are morris men and women who practise their steps from the autumn equinox through to spring in readiness for the May Day celebrations. They then continue to dance outside pubs and in towns and villages all over Britain throughout early summer. The dances have been handed down from generation to generation and have traditional tunes to accompany them. Some morris sides are purely men and others women and some are both. There are dances to welcome spring, increase fertility, raise sexual energy, and generally lift people's spirits. As May was also a time traditionally associated with war, some dances are the literal remnants of our ancestors war dances. There are many traditional costumes and each morris will vary with molly dancers usually being the most outrageous. Sticks, handkerchiefs and bells all play a part in the dances and, although some may find the vision of several hunky men donning virginal white, wearing bells and waving their hankies about as vaguely amusing, anyone who has seen a morris dance will know that the morris tradition encompasses all energy levels of the season including the energy of war. When we relate this practice to tribal dances practised around the world we can see similarities. So regardless of whether you think they are ridiculous, amusing or intriguing they will, I hope, continue to beat in spring and continue the tradition and aid the conservation of our British culture.

Previously in our isles the image of the Green Man had been widely described simply as a '*grotesque*'. The French knew the image as '*la tête de feuilles*' or 'the head of leaves', and the German peoples had a whole range of descriptions for him, but due to her intense and rigorous research Lady Raglan named him the Green Man and that he has been (in these Isles, at least) ever since.

Her much-reproduced conclusion and published description of the archetype can be found in an edition of *Folklore* magazine and states

> *The question is whether there was any figure in real life from which it (the Llangwm example) could have been taken. The answer, I think, is there is only one of sufficient importance, the figure known variously as the Green Man, Jack in the Green, Robin Hood, The King of May and the Garland, who is the central figure in the May day celebrations throughout northern and central Europe.*

This exploration may have given us the familiar title we all now use but it only scratched the surface of his whole being. Much research has been carried out by subsequent writers, and by studying the carvings around the world they have all reached a similar conclusion, the Green Man is more than purely a May Day fertility figure – he is mankind and nature combined on all levels of existence. From the prehistoric cave paintings to the gothic revival the image is found relentlessly in elevated positions on religious and, in some cases, political buildings such as the Houses of Parliament in London.

An interesting observation made by one Canon Albert Radcliffe of Manchester Cathedral is that when they occur they outnumber images of Christ by a staggering twelve to one. The fact that they are found in buildings such as Fountains Abbey in Yorkshire is also surprising considering it was a Cistercian Monastery that forbids the inclusion of any graven images.

There are many theories as to why this image has been included in religious buildings and all differ hugely but could also contain some grains of truth. Some believe he is an early attempt to denounce the wild and primitive side that is within all of us, of which I will say more later on, or alternatively that he may have been conceived to honour this ancient nature spirit. These concepts may not rest easy today, but for our earlier Christian forebears it certainly increased the fear of that which is wild or beastlike, and yet balanced the acceptance of humanity's primal roots. As it evolved, Christianity tried to elevate us above nature and as this caught on the majority collectively raised their opinions of themselves. Or in other words the collective ego jumped up a notch.

> *The previous polytheistic paths were essentially dualistic but the emphasis was on matriarchal instinct utilising nature's power as opposed to enforced patriarchal dependence creating a need to control nature's forces.*

Christ's humanitarian messages of love, tolerance, compassion and understanding are yet to be realised and one could argue that we are entering his global vision now as we begin to question all forms of indoctrination and listen more attentively to the inner divinity. This extremely generalised observation is held in response to the huge resurgence of pure spirit that is currently manifesting, and if we have to encompass this divinity with a name or label then it is our choice as individuals to do so but not necessarily required. People often ask me what 'forces' or deities I work with, which I often find hard to convey. As a practising spiritual person I have walked many paths and actively attracted many personifications but the spirit I feel most connected with is that of nature itself. If I have to define this then I would describe it as 'the life force' or 'great spirit'.

Although it may appear that the Green Man is an image of spring and re-birth he is also directly linked by some with Christ and the resurrection. Christ 'died' in early spring but was re-born, just as nature is. Christian clergy may, no doubt, disagree with this over-simplification of Christ's ultimate sacrifice for humanity but as the symbolism and legacy remains the same, the dispute over his actual survival is probably irrelevant now. The symbolism is none the less relevant. The Egyptian god Osiris and goddess Isis are also likened to this sacrificial cycle for, although Osiris was betrayed by his brother Set and murdered, Isis magically restored him and he too was re-born albeit momentarily but long enough to impregnate his wife and in so doing create Horus their literal Son of God. Our relationship with death is an uncomfortable one and one that many of us never truly come to terms with. We know that as part of nature we die and that our 'seed' or children live on afterwards but one of the questions posed by the Green Man is, 'What else?' A very large proportion of humanity believes in an after life or literal re-birth of the soul. As humans we try to convince ourselves that this 'soul' can transcend this dimension and therefore re-inhabit another physical form. In theory this is possible even at the sub-atomic level and science is very close indeed to proving that consciousness can provably exist outside the confines of the physical form. For thousands of years millions of people have chosen to believe in reincarnation and for those with past-life memories this is perceived as reality. One could argue that this is purely fantasy or whimsical but our ancestral genes may prove otherwise. It could be this connection to our past that provides a clue. Many of the Native American tribes believe in the power of ancestral memory and actively seek it out in order to understand better their lives today, as do the Maori and many other primitive tribal groups. This ancestral link has in some respects been broken here in the West as less emphasis is placed upon revering the dead who are, by and large, tucked away quickly in graves or cremated and rarely visited again as for most of us it is enough that we keep the love alive in our hearts.

We have developed a squeamish attitude to death and, apart from the odd exception between actual death and burial, the dead themselves are not treated with any particular care or respect these days.

The Green Man provides us with a direct link to nature and the inner nature of life even at the consciousness level. This ever-changeable energy reacting to its environment seems chaotic and yet at times patterns emerge and we seek a definitive truth. To know 'all' or see the divine in its entirety is probably futile at this stage of our evolution and something we are unlikely to achieve.

Some people, however, are considered divine channels or 'avatars' but proving this quality is hard to achieve and fairly rare. The genuine articles do seem to have abilities beyond what we would consider the norm and have a direct link with nature's forces and are almost able to 'control' them when required. Merlin may well be such a figure, albeit a mythical one, and one that is difficult to prove conclusively, but he is a durable example of the almost lost art of our own indigenous shamanic practices.

The modern interpretation of the 'Second Coming' could be described as the spiritual return and awareness of spirit forcing us to look honestly at ourselves personally and globally and in so doing we appear to be raising our level of awareness. The following statement could probably resonate with all of us at times.

'*I have judged myself and found myself wanting*'.

This two-edged sword is both light and dark depending on how you view it. On the one hand it implies that I have fallen short of my own expectations and the other is simply 'wanting'. The 'wanting', I believe, is our spirit crying out for a greater connection with Gaia or simply 'The Earth' itself.

One's personal growth or 'Great Work' is unique to each of us but at the same time infinitely comparable; what concerns me is the collective consciousness and how it responds to current events, especially as portrayed to us through the media. If you have the technology try watching the same news story as related by several different countries and a familiar pattern reveals itself. Each country will have subtle and even distinct differences but all reflect the politics and religion of its peoples. Now try looking beneath the façade and observe the similarities and a humanitarian picture unfolds of love in all its aspects. This is the picture that spirit wants us to view more intensely, especially as we draw close to the end of this astrological window of collective opportunity and leave the caring sharing world of Pisces behind.

See the common links and with love and understanding travel onwards.

Were early Christian converts too frightened not to give him life? Now this isn't as crazy as it sounds as it could well have started out as a form of appeasement to the wild spirit or a warning to it that any wild behaviour in church will lead to that energy being entrapped or stifled.

We have as much to fear from our repression of wildness as we do our expression of it.

We need, somehow, to balance the positive aspects of reacting instinctively to our pre-conceived indoctrinations on all levels. By balancing heart and mind we can start to understand each insightful moment as it occurs without over-reacting to any situation.

So how can one balance this wild untamed creature within? By awareness that its darker side has its uses and that sometimes we will have to fight, as it is part of our nature to do this. The trick lies in knowing when one is instigating fear or threat in others and therefore through that awareness try to avoid causing it. If, however, you are faced with a totally unprovoked attack you will deal with it instinctively

9

as best you can and for each of us this will vary. Some will freeze with fear, some will passively accept fate, some try to argue their way out and some defend only once attacked, but some see red and it is the 'red zone' that induces the most fear. In this zone we let our inner beast out unleashed against another and it is often chaotic and has little in the way of respect for life. But it still seems to be a valid part of our make up so we need to understand it better rather than try to suppress it. Martial arts, yoga and meditation are all brilliant ways of getting to safely know your inner beast and manage to balance the dichotomy of wild verses tame. This inner discipline is a training of the wild pure state into a directed force only to be applied as a last resort but can be intelligently applied and effective. I'm not suggesting we all run off and join up at the local karate school, as there are many other ways in which one can safely come into contact with your wilder bits. Sex is one such outlet and one that most of us are likely to experience. My own personal morals are directed into sacred and spiritual union but each of us is our own conscience and therefore for many the sexual re-revolution was a turning point of freedom and liberation. Personally, I understand and accept that what consenting adults do to each other is very much their own business. But if we reflect upon sex as a global economic manifestation it seems to be our favourite subject, albeit still tainted with taboos.

Considering there seem to be no perimeters to a wild state, that in itself concerns us as we know only too well how far the boundaries of human behaviour can go. We understand that, in some cases, extreme suppression of desire can lead to perversion and indeed harmful actions. Modern psychology is trying to understand this but extreme compassion and understanding is arguably wasted on some whose wilder parts have focused so intently upon destruction to others. We still have a long way to go.

The Victorian wake of this sexual suppression still haunts many of us and can restrict our individual experiences, as do negative intimate moments. It is still a subject we feel we should behave instinctively about and for many talking about it is almost seen as failure or inhibiting. We grow up thinking we should just be able 'to do it' and that it will all come naturally, which for many it does but not all. The current boom in sexual counsellors and pornography reflects both our inner repressions and outer manifestations of desire. We are all extremes sexually and that in itself is scary. One could argue that the extreme light of sex is to transcend it and many mystics, religions and spiritual paths advocate this chaste life of purity but very few people honestly achieve it and I'm not convinced they are that enlightened or chaste. It is a little publicised fact that many early Christian monks and nuns did in fact marry and it was only the Catholic Church that altered this course. Even then it was fairly common for indiscretions as many monasteries and nunneries occupied close quarters and one can still see much evidence for this today in parts of the world. We holidayed in Corfu many times as children and one cannot help but notice the close proximity of the Island monastery and its sister the nunnery on shore. This particular combination is found all over northern Europe and one cannot imagine it was for any other reason.

You have to travel past the nunnery to get the boat out to the monastery. This puts temptation squarely under their respective noses.

We are led by our inner beast when drawn sexually towards another and often don't consciously acknowledge these desires until the beast has worked its magic. Pheromones, primal visual expectations, body language, flirting, and peacock behaviour all occur well before we are aware of it. By then it is usually too late to inflict any rational thought over the matter as seeds have been sown by nature's inner energies. Many people then transcend to a period of what I describe as 'brain sex' and will put their best 'face' forward in an attempt to consolidate that which their hormones are already screaming at them to do. The veil of love is created and during this 'courtship' period much magic occurs. Links and coincidences are logged by the mind whilst nature just continues to allure until eventually the couple reach a moment of make or break. For some this whole process can take nanoseconds, for others much longer, years even. Each of us works in our own way and responds to our own inner 'wyrd' or energy.

If we turn about-face here from light to dark we realise the extreme outcomes of denying the inner beast and its cumulative effects.

All social and religious groups have experienced public humiliation and embarrassment at times by some of their followers' arcane activities coming to light, and it is well known that for those with reasonably normal or high sex drives suppression can pervert the beast into a harmful or destructive force. But for most of us free sexual expression isn't a harmful or perverse activity – it is a natural act of intimacy and love through which our spirits can join and dance in mutual harmony. It can be one of the few ways in which we can unleash our primitive side in relative safety, unwanted pregnancies and STDs aside. It is also a time when we feel at our most vulnerable and therefore we equate it with birth and death.

All forms of creation will allow 'safe' expression of wildness but to deny this will sicken the spirit and leave people with negative expression as their only outlet.

This leads us straight back to our friend the Green Man and his role as exemplifier of nature's rhythms. Many of the pagan traditions and influences of our past have been attributed to this image. The Celtic/ Germanic horned god Cernunnos represents the male energy of wild and natural woodland. He rises anew each spring as a young stag or fresh buds, the results of last year's union, and calls lovers to his spaces to dance. By 1 May his energy is at its height and he is ready to give his fertility for the coming season. Traditionally this was a time for 'fucking or fighting' as one Anglo-Saxon informed me recently and there is certainly evidence in Celtic traditions for it being the most common time for going to war. The more peaceful would feast and pair off, running into the woods to have sex under the influence of this wild energy. It is believed that ancient customs like this are held responsible for prejudice against paganism today as Christians likened these activities to devilish orgiastic behaviour. This unfounded belief probably owes more of its origin to Mediterranean practices than to our native roots. By summer he slows down, taking it easy, and encourages us to enjoy the splendour of his bounty by resting in lush fields and appreciating nature's rich bounty soon to be harvested. The spirit of John Barleycorn is celebrated in crop growing parts of Britain as the Corn God – he is cut down but re-grows each spring. John Barleycorn means 'heart of the barley' and is also celebrated as a god of brewing. He is yet another link or representation of the Green Man. Corn dollies or little gods and goddesses are traditionally made at this time and the methods have become quite sophisticated over the years. There is indeed much patience and skill required when creating corn dollies but as with any creative desire the energy put in will provide one with some form of satisfaction and greater understanding of harvest and sacrifice. As autumn approaches he is busy again gathering in the harvest for which we traditionally give thanks. As we thank nature for her bounty so the Green Man says thanks in his own unique way by giving us the stunning autumn colours and the whole of the country gradually becomes testament to the marriage of spring and fertility of his union with the goddess. As winter draws in he protects himself and becomes a spirit of ideas and inspiration, gradually thinning the veil and allowing us access to the dead.

This ancient nature spirit is one we are all familiar with but know by another name, the Devil. Why was he given this title? Well probably because he is the direct link to that which is still wild and free inside us all. He knows no boundaries and rebels against convention. The world of Christian indoctrination, or any dogma for that matter, has no place in his dimension. All expressions are valid and much creativity results from meeting our friend the Horned God. I did a meditation once many years back to ask this spirit why he was seen as 'devilish' and his message to me on the much-publicised negative aspect of his character was

'You have nothing to fear except fear itself'.

Read that again.

Dionysus, Greek god of the vine or grapes, is often portrayed in such a manner although his myths are better known. Born one of the twelve Olympian gods, Dionysus became the intoxicated god of ecstasy and uninhibited revelry. Having been brought up in a wild cave after Zeus hid his whereabouts from the vengeful Hera he discovered the art of brewing and making wine. This he taught to man, who has had to live with it ever since. Those gods who refused to acknowledge his divine status were either driven mad or killed themselves and so we see the darker side of alcohol rearing its ugly head. Ironically Hera and Dionysus eventually became reconciled and she elevated his godly presence with her approval. There are many, many myths and legends connected to Dionysus but his Green Man attributes are there nonetheless. He is a wild spirit of forgotten places, he lives instinctively and bravely, he is thought responsible for theatre and/or acting in general, he is a god of excesses but his myths of death and self torture and ultimate destruction warn us of the dangers of following his path too closely.

Silvanus, Roman god of woodland and deer, is a close relation to Dionysus and has similar attributes but is more akin to an elder Pan and lacks Dionysus's extreme behaviour. Seen as a gentle aged shepherd he watches over his flocks whilst enjoying the wild wood and its energies also.

Pan, the Greek equivalent to Cernunnos, was strongly associated with the wild wood. Homer's poem to Pan states that he was born of an unnamed daughter of Dryops and sired by Hermes but like so many claims of myth and legend this is again a disputed mythology. For our benefit it is interesting to note that although he embodies the wildness of nature and is its true nature, early attempts at denouncement by Christianity encouraged people to face this as an adversary. By process of extremes – by drunkenness, gluttony and sexual excess or denial of physical pleasures – one would face one's inner primal fears and meet Pan. He was then seen as tempter or devilish in the eyes of the beholder. To resist this was seen as transcendent and proof of one's ability to resist evil. And yet to be filled with his glory is actually very self empowering and as beautiful as the nature he is. As I write this I am allowing his energy to flow and find it funny that so much fear is associated with such love. Pure and unconditional, it fills every pore – urging me to be at peace with wildness; and yet his ecstasy lifts me, strengthening my faith and trust in nature. As we reach up to this almost unattainable 'heaven' we fear that which lies under our feet and view it as 'hell'. The origins of this 'hell' are, as many already know, stolen from the northern or heathen traditions and 'hell' itself is Hel, the deity or goddess of the underworld. The ultimate result of death and decay of organic matter, whether it be human, animal or vegetable, is re-absorption into the earth or below ground level and so it relates to the underworld. This underworld was once perceived as a place of rejuvenation or re-birth but has since been corrupted into the concept of a dreadful 'hellish' place. As mortals we have given ourselves this dichotomy of suspension higher than nature yet lower than divinity and yet it was never meant to be that way. We stay in this grey void of uselessness unable to directly connect with either aspects of our true nature. Pan is, much like all of his kind, an energy of raw and wild nature through which we can become the key to portals of all dimensions. Pan is believed by many, and Horace was no exception, to be a lonely god – and as the goat wanders, picking his way carefully through the night cannily playing his pipes, his is a sad tale of unrequited love and his force was often likened to Apollo. They competed musically and it is said that one such encounter held Pan as the better musician, angering Apollo, who gave him an ass's ears as a punishment. He has a reputation for lustful advances towards the nymphs of the woods some of whom ran in fear from his advances and others, such as Selene, reciprocated. His song is therefore one of love in all its extremes.

Female deities also link in with wilder aspects of the Green Man. The huntress goddess, Diana, originated from Italy but has links with other deities such as Artemis (Greek) and Selene all of whom portray the wild instinctive side of femininity. Allegedly Diana was celebrated by a specific Diana cult by the shores of Lake Nemi in a grove. The lake was thought to be Diana's mirror. The god Virbius and a nymph, Egeria, were also worshipped here in conjunction with Diana. One could say the male and female consorts were her vessels for humanity. The associations we are most interested in are hunting and her preference for wild places. This places her well and truly in Green Man territory where in truth the huntress can become the hunted.

The majority rarely encounters this primal fear of literally becoming something else's dinner these days but for some it is reality. Game wardens, adventurers, hunters, zoo keepers etc. all expose themselves to this risk but in truth we have more to fear from each other today than being consumed in a literal sense by primitive beasties. Diana is also a goddess of birth, balancing the paradigm and elevating her to true mother status.

Artemis, the parallel Greek goddess of hunting, varies little from her Roman archetype. She is linked with purity, hunting, the wild wood, the Moon and childbirth. Her complex mythology is difficult to condense but suffice it to say she encompasses that which is young, virginal and brave in women. Her destructive side is utilised in the 'hunt', this earthly practice of necessity. She is generous and kind to the young but deals out death and hardship to 'those who should know better'. Only Hera (wife of Zeus) ever gets the better of her. In Homer's *Battle of the Gods*, she fares badly in Hera's hands and runs crying to her father like a spoilt child and I suspect there is an element of this in Artemis. She is definitely portrayed as one who likes to get her own way and is fiercely competitive.

Selene was known to the Romans as Luna or the Moon and also has links to Diana, Artemis and the Green Man. Pan was thought to be one of her lovers and she bestowed him with a fine fleece. She rides the heavens in her chariot driven by illustrious horses from the east at mid-month or when the moon is full.

And now we touch upon fear, for there are deities linked with the Green Man that only the foolish or intrepid work with. At least that's what two thousand years of Christianity would have us believe. As it is they were probably perverted interpretations and one such character is Loki, the Nordic trickster god, the twinkle in the corner of the eye, the wicked grin, the mask and general mischief maker. Hollywood acclaimed him with their film *The Mask* and Jim Carrey did him some justice. The film *Dogma* also gave us its rendition and although I wasn't hugely convinced of the choice of actor for the role his attributes were well shown. Fear of this faceless god is understandable. I was but five when he made his first appearance during dream time. It terrified me to the primal core. As he removed each mask another appeared and I realised this spirit could be found in many places at once. Not an easy one for one so young to deal with and not something I could tell my parents. We should all talk to kids about dreams, openly. Now I realise it was our mutual fear reflected.

The Loki twinkle blends a strong seductive draw with an almost forbidden element to it. In my experience Loki is just when he feels it is right to be so but untameable and unpredictable in extremes at times. Loki people – and I say people, as he frequently works through women too – are usually rebellious and naughty but keep it up their sleeves as they are cunning and possess a rare genius for solving complex issues. He is also linked to wolves who prefer a woodland home. But at the first sign of real danger he is off.

Lilith is much revered by many today, particularly by feminist pagans as an aspect of the dark Goddess, but the composite modern deity seems to have been drawn from many roots. The mythological Sumerian *lilu/lilitu* demon of wild places encompasses male and female attributes and appears to have joined forces with the Jewish Lilith, a rebellious female thought to be Adam's first wife. In some versions of the Epic of Gilgamesh she is mentioned as a wild spirit that has taken hold of a willow tree and has an owl of wisdom nesting above in the branches with a snake sleeping below. The tree is sacrificed by Gilgamesh who causes the spirit living within it to take flight. This myth bears more resemblance to Innana/Istar and her link with sacred trees than with the original Lilith.

This symbolic sacrifice marked a significant time for women when their lives were literally about to be re-defined over night. Agriculture and domestication united nature and women in a mutual fear not ever experienced before. Men could now chop down trees with axes and women were about to be relegated to domestic breeding machines and homemakers. The Hebrew story is quite different and portrays her as a stubborn and rebellious woman who refuses Adam's advances, so angering God who banishes her to forgotten caves. They held her responsible for all stillbirths and deaths of boys under eight. She was also thought to be the perpetrator of wet dreams. I dispute this, as does she, but the fears are thousands of years old and therefore well established and so it follows that an aspect of this energy has manifested into just which the Hebrews most feared.

Most women who work with Lilith may have problems unless they are barren but I have found her a most empowering and inspiring energy on the whole but she certainly invokes fear in others – a downside I hadn't considered until recently.

I personally believe that the early blending of Christianity and paganism met with some conciliatory gestures such as letting the spirit of nature into their sacred spaces. Considering most early churches were built in part if not entirely out of wood this makes sense.

It is believed that many churches and cathedrals were built on sites we believe to have been sacred in some way to our pagan ancestors but this is disputable. The first obvious markings of sacred spaces referred to the graves of ancestors so it follows that these were special places to which people could go to commune with the spirits of their deceased relatives. They may well have included a few sacred groves along the way, if such places ever really existed. These 'groves' were not only places of magical energy as in wells or clusters of trees but the people themselves were the grove in my eyes. Perhaps they felt that by integrating the actual trees themselves into the buildings they had taken this spirit with them? Out of reverence, or a need for control, the faces are fixed in place, looking down upon the parishioners. This 'taming' of the old beliefs could be part of the original reason but why do they occur so universally and frequently? Was it to mark our destiny in conjunction with the new Christian era ahead, maybe? I prefer to think it was acknowledgement of the powerful forces of nature and a reminder that **we ignore these at our own peril**. But if we are to believe this to be the only answer why do they continue to occur throughout history? It is possible that it became a tradition continued without question but I doubt that, as humans by nature question everything.

The construction of the first churches offered everyone in the community a chance to meet together under one roof. They came to worship an essentially human saviour in a dry and equal place. This concept taken on, they enjoyed the benefits of a simplified monotheistic practice in a multi-purpose building.

The Green Man's origins are evident in all the earliest belief systems around the world especially in forested or once-forested areas where our ancestors' relationship with trees was most interdependent. This was because you could actually meet him. The arrival of Christianity really did start to change all this. The structure of Christianity attempted to move people away from their nature-based, personified polytheistic past into its patriarchal monotheistic future. This became a more consumable society where the ethos was now on gaining wealth for the newly formed Church. The mere concept of meeting our friend The Green Man and experiencing his unlimited natural love didn't rest easy with the dictates of the new ethos. The lives of our ancestors at this time were based on group survival and daily manual work for all but the elite. The Church had to find ways of selling the idea of building their churches and clearing more land in a way that might be acceptable to the potential converts. We have very little documented history of this time and it is generally accepted amongst historians that there was a gradual assimilation that strengthened and grew more autocratic in nature. This then led on to a deliberate purge of heathen behaviour and the subsequent emergence of the Catholic Church. It's interesting to note here that pagans treated early Christians in much the same way initially so the cycle of fear has repeated itself.

These people had mostly related spiritually to their deities in the open air or in their homes so the whole concept of a separate communal sacred building was a very modern innovation. A powerful story that reflects this time well is that of St. Amand and the blind woman. She, a pagan, is asked by a bishop to take an axe and cut down a tree. As she raises her axe two heads rise up from the crown of the tree, aghast at what she is doing. She couldn't see this of course. Then the bishop blesses her, telling her to continue, which she does. Immediately her sight is restored, a miracle attributed to St. Amand. Christianity was sold to the people on the premise that a new way must be seen and this woman's sight was proof that they were right. It is interesting to note that during his lifetime five centuries earlier St. Amand was responsible for the destruction of many groves of oak. I personally believe that they stemmed from stone age clearings that animals are drawn to for a variety of reasons. Hunters could easily observe these spaces and it would have been quite easy pickings I think. I have sat on the edge of one such place on many occasions to wait for deer and they rarely let me down. Deer are naturally curious animals so easily caught out. This knowledge and wisdom is still practised today by the deer cullers of coppiced woodland. By creating the modern equivalent of a sacred space with several straight short rides the hunter can sit above it all in his tree chair and pick off the one he has chosen. This less barbaric method of killing the deer is only really suitable for dense woodland, which is why we see alternative methods employed by country folk in differing terrains. The most interesting development during the dark ages that affected people's changing relationship with trees was the invention of the heavy plough. This made more extensive agriculture and larger fields now viable and was very attractive to those who worked on the earth. It's important to realise that at this time most of the population were hunters, animal domesticators and farmers. During the Iron Age great technological advances were made and the development of ploughs, axes, and all other 'new' agricultural tools enabled people to cut down larger trees for the first time. Although it is nice to think they would have deemed some as 'special' or 'sacred', it's not provable. The new religion seduced them but just like the belief system it was replacing it had its own dark side, which manifested itself fairly quickly. This patriarchal divine being was pretty typical of any father: if you did well in his eyes he rewarded you or tested you, presumably depending on what he felt was required. At times, so the Old Testament states, he was a genocidal maniac not averse to the utilisation of nature's power to punish whole cities if he deemed it necessary. These ancient Hebrew stories must have rung bells in early converts' heads as they too had gods with huge destructive powers. Any localised natural catastrophe could be accredited to one or more of these forces and was often seen as a direct sign that they as a community had done wrong in someone's eyes and had to be punished. The extreme light and dark that constituted these composite divinities continues to this day, as does the belief in a 'greater power than man' and in spite of our increasing scientific knowledge of the world we live in we are no closer now to gaining any form of absolute control over this power than we were thousands of years ago. There are, I know, many scientific people who will disagree with me on this but even with our so called 'advances' genetically we are foolishly stabbing in the dark. We live in constantly changing times and like the spirit of the Green Man we have to adapt and overcome in order to survive. Nature is the most powerful force and no amount of interference, destruction, control or love will change this fact. Whether we as a race survive matters little to the elemental forces but to the Green Man it does for he cannot exist without us and we without him.

By medieval times stone masonry was already an established craft and carpentry had leapt on in bounds. This made the building of larger barns and religious buildings a more viable proposition. For the remaining practitioners of nature-based beliefs this must have been a time of deep concern of the possible repercussions of such a sudden change in their environment. The so called 'dark ages' or transitional phase spiritually and globally was probably in truth a very exciting time to live, with change constantly round every corner − that is, if you like change. Great advances were made and our lives became far more complex as a result. One could liken it to the period we have been in since the industrial revolution. As we created the picture postcard landscape of patchwork fields and thatched cottages a new England began to emerge with a king in every county. This gradual assimilation of communities to larger groups paved the way for the eventual 'dragon wars' fought to establish the United Kingdom of Scotland, Wales and England that we have today.

It also marked a time when we began to distance ourselves from the whites of each other's eyes in combat. As we softened and tamed ourselves domestically in one direction so we became squeamish of battle and to some extent hunting too. With the introduction of armour, cannon, longer bows and eventually gun shot we attempted to sidestep confrontation in the form of better defences. What's left of our medieval castles are a permanent reminder of these territorial fights. One wonders what a knight of such times would make of modern warfare? The quintessential Green Man is neither warrior nor peace maker − he is essentially disinterested in such mortal behaviour unless it threatens him, which it now does.

His explosive arrival during early church building marked another such time, for as our ancestors threatened his spirituality so he redressed the issue by inspiration for whatever reason and consolidated his 'face' for all to see.

> *As the tree is sown*
> *I wait for the light*
> *As the tree grows*
> *I wait for the fight*
> *As the tree struggles*
> *I wait for insight*
> *As the tree dies*
> *I wait for the night*

The already mentioned Celtic/Germanic tree god Cernunnos is shown in one case on the famous Gundestrap cauldron, found in Germany, with hair of leaves and holding up two deer symbolic of the wild wood. He often portrayed as a wild horned god leaping about woodland and is often associated with oak. The oak tree is probably one of our most loved native species and also with the exception of yew has greatest longevity. The mere thought of the Major Oak of Sherwood and others like it having survived since the tail end of the dark ages is phenomenal. What tales those trees can tell.

The legend of Windsor Park's Herne the Hunter, although not symbolic of the Green Man himself, is still very much a part of his environment if the sightings of this unfortunate spirit are to be believed. His first appearance in literature is in Shakespeare's *The Merry Wives of Windsor* although he is thought to have evolved from an older folklore of Richard II's time. It is believed that a character called Herne (or something like it) once worked in Windsor Great Park as a huntsman for the king but was unpopular with his peer group due to his prowess and regal favouritism, so they ensnared him in a foul trap. Accompanied by his two black hounds he was always chosen to lead the great hunt. On one such occasion the king and Herne were in pursuit of a particularly fine stag with huge antlers and found themselves separated from the rest of the field. The stag stood its ground and then charged at the king's horse, goring it and causing the king to fall. Almost instantly, so it is told, Herne threw himself between the stag and the king and received a near-fatal wound but managed to deal the stag a lethal blow, stabbing it with his knife. Distraught, the king promised Herne that, should he survive, he would promote him to head huntsman – but Herne was dying and cared little for this offer.

King Richard called for the rest of the hunt and proclaimed that if anyone could save Herne's life they would be greatly rewarded, but they were secretly pleased with the outcome and said he should be left to die. Suddenly a stranger on a black horse appeared and approached the king, saying he was skilled in medicine and could heal Herne. The king, suspicious of this stranger and mistaking him for a poacher, asked him to identify himself, which he did, claiming to be one Philip Urswick from Bagshot Common. Richard gave the stranger the benefit of the doubt and allowed him to proceed with his healing work. First Urswick instructed that the antlers of the stag be removed and placed upon Herne's head, and then organised his extradition from the woods to his hut. The jealous huntsmen moaned continually about Herne, to the point where Urswick asked them what they would be prepared to give should he interfere with the healing process.

Stumped for ideas, they simply promised to do the first thing asked of them by Urswick in one month's time, when Herne would be fully recovered. In return for this Urswick declared Herne would no longer be able to practise his woodworking or hunting skills. The prophecy came true one month later and although Herne was kept in the best of lodgings in the castle itself he lost all his previous skills and the king lost interest in supporting his recovery further. The other huntsmen could also do no good and became dismayed at how everyone's luck seemed to have changed since the incident. Herne left the castle in a deranged state and was later found hanging from an oak tree by a pedlar. That very night, it is said, a flash of lightning struck the tree, now known as Herne's Oak, in a terrible thunderstorm. The worried huntsmen called Urswick back to solve their bewitchment and he instructed them to go to Herne's Oak and wait for Herne to appear. The ghost of Herne did indeed make an appearance and told them to ride with him in the wild hunt. This enchanted motley crew wreaked havoc upon the king's forest, infuriating the monarch. Eventually the king travelled to the haunted tree and demanded to speak with the ghost of Herne, who obligingly made his presence felt. The king asked Herne why he haunted the park and led his huntsmen astray. Herne replied that it was his vengeance and that only the hanging of the jealous keepers would avenge his life. The king did as he was bid and suffered no more at the hands of Herne.

There have been several sightings since and it is thought he only appears to warn of impending disaster to the Royal family. There are many other versions of this story but this one remains the most popular. All seem to include some sort of excessive behaviour relating to hunting and involve the wearing of the antlers by Herne. One story involves the defilement of a virgin by Herne and his punishment but all are infinitely refutable.

There is also a link between Herne and the appearance of a white stag portending danger or death. The character of Herne resounds profoundly with shamanic practices and one can see a direct comparison between the archetype of the Horned God and the symbiosis of man and deer.

Numerous accounts of spiritual or special trees and their relationship with people abound. Alexander the Great is supposed to have been warned not to travel any farther into India on one occasion by a tree whose trunk was made of snakes and whose fruit was the heads of women. Another version of supposedly the same story tells of him meeting the Tree of the Sun and the Tree of the Moon: he is told to kiss the Tree of the Sun first by daylight and ask a question then wait until morning to ask the Tree of the Moon a question. He does as requested and both trees give a gloomy outlook, again warning him that to proceed will be very dangerous and this time, more specifically, he would have to deal with some treachery. The god who allowed this information to come his way was thought to have been Dionysus or Bacchus.

Buddha received his most enlightened moments whilst sat under trees. According to *The Light of Asia*, by Edwin Arnold, he is 'discovered' by his people sitting under a Bodhi tree by the banks of the river Phalgu, a much revered site for pilgrims, and later it is said he instructed Prince Siddartha to sit under a jamba tree to 'listen', indicating that the tree has some direct connection or significance in his teachings. The prince's own personal 'path' started in the extreme luxury and comfort of an over-protected environment and he was initially shocked to discover pain and suffering for the first time. This led him to literally go walk-about throughout his land in search of answers to the problems facing humanity. As a prince he felt it was his duty and also his destiny. Each of his steps to enlightenment are marked by him sitting, not seeking but just open and listening to the inner wisdom whilst under a tree.

> *So, saying the good Lord Buddha seated him*
> *Under a jamba tree, with ankles crossed*
> *As holy statues sit and first begin*
> *To meditate this deep disease of life,*
> *What its far source and whence its remedy*
> *So vast a pity filled him, such wide love*
> *For living things, such passion to heal pain,*
> *That by their stress his princely spirit passed*
> *To ecstasy, and, purged from mortal taint*

Of sense and self, the boy attained thereat
Dhyana, first step of 'the path'.

I certainly haven't studied Buddhism in any great detail but it would make sense to me that the spirit of nature or our friend the Green Man bestowed his 'knowing' or enlightened this moment of clarity.

Christ also received such insight when meditating in nature's beauty, and the Garden of Gethsemane is one such place to which he turned, albeit allegedly at Mary Magdalene's invitation. It is believed by many that he 'saw' his own 'end' here and although he initially faltered he stuck with it as he also witnessed his own resurrection and subsequent legacy to mankind. One would like to think that the spirit of nature gave him the inner strength to go forth and meet his future as a potential saviour. His journey into the 'wilderness' for forty days and nights was also a form of communion with nature's wilder forces. In this inhospitable place he is said to have been tempted by the 'devil' or as I prefer to think his own inner weaknesses. He avoided this road of least resistance and in so doing was further enlightened and energised. This self-perpetuated torture is common to many spiritual paths as initiates put themselves through extremes to strengthen will and gain absolute control over their inner selves. This increased spiritual strength overrides the physical plane and allows people to transcend pain and suffering in themselves and others. It is often accompanied by a bestowed gift or divine insight or message pertinent to their individual path. Many 'religions' owe their 'roots' to man communing with trees or being in such an environment.

Many members of today's Jesus Christ Church of Latter-day Saints or Mormons are quiet about their founder's origins and connections with the occult world. Joseph Smith is believed, amongst other things, to have practised the reading of runes and was also known for his vast amounts of time spent in woodland seeing visions. This direct contact with magical energies spurred him on to found one of the largest religious movements of the twentieth and twenty-first century. It doesn't take much to imagine what was going on there!

There are so many tales and accounts of spiritual, religious and magical connections with woodlands that a comprehensive global book on the subject would probably result in a complete set of encyclopaedias, so we can only touch on a few.

Looking at some of the more down-to-earth peasant practices or 'root' magical tree workings, their simplicity is often the key to their effectiveness.

In this country we have a well-established practice and an almost instinctive draw to leaving offerings on trees or by them. These 'clootie' trees are usually found in special or magical spots all over the country and often have ribbons, jewellery and other less salubrious 'offerings' tied to or left by them by people. The practice of 'wishing trees' and 'wishing wells' is common in these isles and could theoretically go back quite a considerable time. The idea is basic and simple: it involves direct contact with the spirit of the tree or well by being in its presence. Simply by showing reverence and making your wish and expressing inwardly or outwardly your desire it manifests into reality.

During the early medieval period, the custom of forming lead or silver into leaf shapes with wishes engraved upon them was allegedly used for spells, curses etc., and throwing them into pools or springs was practised in certain areas. This tradition is thought to have originated from Italy but similar practices using the image of a leaf as an offering are found in various parts of the world. Here in Britain there is an old custom of picking a willow leaf and wearing it in your hat for a month after breaking up with a loved one. This apparently prevents you harbouring negative thoughts over your lost love and helps attract a new one should you so wish. Romanies also used willow magic in love spells, by throwing up to nine shoes into a willow tree until one shoe stuck. This assured you of success in love. Many shoes, good odds.

Farther afield in Brazil is the spirit named Curupia who resides in the rain forests. He has green teeth and green feet with his heels facing the front so that anyone trying to track him would always be going in the opposite way. This equivocal aspect of the Green Man is often a deliberate desire of spirit to mislead or allow you to get 'lost' amongst it rather than instigating rational thought when in his territory. It certainly would have taught hunters the value of not leaving a trail for others to follow but it also enticed them to follow their own inner beat rather than emulating.

> *The collective results of man's achievements are the culmination of his sensory perceptions in relationship and attempted mimicry of his environment.*
> *Or; All that we are is all we have ever perceived from nature.*
> *We are poor mimics.*
> *Does the gecko create paint to don his body with when required?*
> *No.*

So was the image of the Green Man purely for luck and protection or were there deeper roots? Obviously there are.

We know that there was a transitional pagan/Christian period religiously. We also know that many traditions were blended, stolen and in some cases forgotten at this time.

When the first churches were built most of them were constructed from wood and it is likely that the early builders of these structures were pagan or early converts. Trees had as great an importance then as they do now but we were individually more intimate with trees and their uses a thousand years ago than we are now. They were and still are the main source of shelter, furniture, heating and ships, not to mention their healing properties and inspirational qualities; and maybe out of reverence and respect a whole belief system was based on them.

There are some documented cases of the more important sacred groves but the majority would have been less obvious. Most of the ancestors prior to Christianity revered their local spirits firstly as they were the ones they literally connected with. By tuning into the energy of their local special places, wells and groves etc they became aware of the uniqueness each place had and identified with this energy, whilst it mixed in neatly with their own wyrd. How often have you been somewhere and either felt, 'I know this place' or at the other extreme, 'I don't know why but I don't feel happy or comfortable here'?

So when exactly did this relationship with trees begin? If we journey back in time to our earliest upstanding ancestor we meet Lucy, a member of the *Australopithecus afarensis*, our earliest examples of a bipedal hominoid. We all originate from apes: this we know, but do you know just how many millennia our ancestors lived in and among trees? According to anthropologists it was about two to three million years – that would account for over half of man's existence here on Earth. Most modern *Homo sapiens* left Africa due to a massive change in climate caused by volcanic activity that turned a once entirely forested area into the place we now recognise, more or less. As food and shelter became scarce we spread east, north and west and found new forests to live, scavenge, hunt and shelter in, adapting to circumstances and overcoming drought and hunger as we went. One could argue that each global catastrophe marks yet another leap in evolution and in some respects induces initiation. Most of our northern European ancestors lived in these forests. We are drawn to them for one simple reason: the habitat suits us and meets our requirements as living creatures on this planet. If we then imagine our entire human history as represented by a year we have only spent about three or four months of our time living away from trees. The adaptable migrants to our shores (possibly early Picts and Celts from Europe) brought their tools and industry with them and may or

25

may not have encountered indigenous Britons living in woodland. Efforts to live along side each other would have proved explosive as the two groups relied on differing resource needs. One needed land to grow crops the other required woodland to hunt beasts. These wild untamed humans would have been greatly feared by the new inhabitants and yet many were possibly absorbed over time through breeding whilst others died out from encountering new diseases and lack of food. I emphasise that this is all speculation and many archaeologists and historians may well disagree with this theory but modern DNA testing is showing up higher levels of Neanderthal and Cro Magnon genes in certain areas of Britain, especially close to ancient woodland.

We can look at most of the older and naturally evolved cities we have constructed over the last few thousand years and see them as great forests too, albeit concrete ones. Evolution as we know operates on the system of survival of the fittest dependent on what the climatic and resource conditions are in relation to the life forms requirements for reproduction. This is why there is so much diversity of life in forests. Cities reflect this with their wide variety of buildings, roads and parks all having evolved through our needs and collective demands. As some of the old buildings decay so new ones replace them. Occasionally, as in forests, a fire or catastrophe can befall them and great purged areas are laid bare for future development. Old cities are a glorious conglomeration of old and new buildings of ever-varying size and design, just like forests. London has got to be one of the best examples of this and is also one of the greenest cities you could come across. Although it was once part of a great forest it still has many elements of that forest remaining today. As well as this modern analogy we can still see evidence for its forested past. The majestic Thames flows through it, fed by many tributaries along the way supplying the water element. London has many great parks and many great trees to explore, most of which are considered sacred by their users supplying the tree element.

Just to the northeast of London we have Epping Forest, a place known for Green Man sightings having inspired the likes of Dick Turpin that we will explore in greater detail later in the book. Its southern boundary is on the edge of the 'East End' at Forest Gate and the northern boundary is in Epping or Thornwood Common.

Royal Parks such as Greenwich Park are believed to be protected from development due to their link with the Goddess energy securing 'power spots' that help safeguard the area as a whole.

We still have a primeval relationship with the forest and instinctively emulate the environment from which we evolved. It is this most ancient of roots that I feel proves our inextricable link with forests and, possibly, our earliest awareness of the spirit of the Green Man. In my eyes this spirit could well have been the first divinity our ancestors made connections with, hence making the Green Man our oldest reverence or root of all subsequent deities and divinities. This belief can in part be proved by our increased understanding of anthropology and for some an instinctive understanding of nature's spirit in its raw state. This presumption will be challenged, and indeed refuted by many I'm sure, but I believe it to be true and also feel that very soon the many scientists now investigating our history will soon declare such a notion as absolute.

As our environment changes so we place sacred influence on those special or magical places we have left and in so doing create conservation and a need for it.

Over several cycles trees or 'groves' – and I use the term loosely – can begin to feel magical and special, probably due to the energy created within them. The one I frequent is used all season by deer for a variety of purposes. In Autumn they mate. In winter they strip bark off saplings and dig water holes if dry. In early spring the adult males shed their antlers. Around Beltane or soon after they give birth in them. In early summer they sleep out of the sun of their more exposed grazing patches. In early autumn they are alert and fighting for real and sadly we cull them. The use of the grove increased in its uniqueness and energy. I think it is a misconception to imagine that our ancestors used these places for religious purposes. From the archaeology left it seems that the border lands or no-man's-land between tribes was more commonly utilised. As these were often places unsuitable for growing crops and/or grazing animals it made sense that they would be suitable resting spots for the dead. From what we can tell the earliest group ritual acts were burials. By the time of the Great Stone Circles, burials had become big events and people had moved away from burying their family under their roundhouses to placing them in specially marked spots on neutral territory. It is possible, therefore, that many of the older standing stones are nothing more than tombstones. If we look back five thousand years and before we see an almost universal method of burial emerging. Small round pits were dug, into which the deceased were placed. I have a new theory on this practice and how it came about. Our nomadic ancestors would have family members fall ill and die but what did they do with the seriously sick or injured when it came time to move on? I believe burial pits were originally healing or dying pits. If a member of your group was unable to walk they became a hazard to the others by slowing you down and therefore far more vulnerable to attack. By placing your injured, sick or dying family member in a special pit complete with their possessions and some food and water they created a womb-like hospital. You handed responsibility of your kind over to the spirit of the underworld who would make its decision one way or another. By marking these spots in some way they could find them again. Maybe if some people were spared a stone could be placed to mark this magical spot that would then be seen as potentially a place of healing magic. Once mankind became aware of re-incarnation so the tradition expanded with the Egyptians being the most elaborate of practitioners. The deceased were buried along with any possessions they may need in their journey through the underworld.

The natural eroded resurrection of 'Sea Henge' on the north Norfolk coast at Holme in this country during the 1990s made quite an impression on those aware of it and the media created its usual circus once archaeologists decided to move it. This circle of ancient tree stumps enclosed a larger upturned stump. There are many other natural stumps or stools across the beach still evident, making us think that the area was once forested. There are several theories as to its original usage, ranging from the deathbed either of a special person, or potentially a dangerous one, but as no remains have been excavated it is dubious. One very good, and I feel likely, explanation for its origins is the supposition of it being a place to 'lay' the dead. This theory stands investigation as the era of its construction is indeed prehistoric and therefore ties in with practices of the time. If we accept that people no longer buried their dead at home then a special place would need to be found. It soon became evident to our ancestors that the death process or rotting down of bodies was exceptionally unpleasant and a health risk to have contact with. By laying a body out in a neutral safe place the elements and nature's forces could literally strip the carcass down to the bones. These could then be buried ritualistically. It also made the task easier when the ground was simply too hard to dig. So by leaving the dead protected in a magical circle they ensured that the bones would still be there when ready for burial. This practice could also be carried out in 'special spots' knowing that death induced fear and would deter any alien human intervention from other tribes.

Rites of passage were very much offered by the new church and many of the old ways were incorporated especially where birth, marriage and death are concerned. With its newly created parish records and enclosed graveyards the church offered permanent immortality to all who could afford it. One such practice taken from the old ways is the custom of growing yew trees in churchyards. The yew was a tree of protection, in part due to its resistance and longevity but also probably because of its poisonous qualities. Yew trees live longer than any other of our native species and therefore were and still are associated with immortality. Its evergreen presence both encapsulates the resurrection and afterlife with its seemingly eternal life. The building of churches offered everyone in the community the chance to praise a human saviour in a dry and equal place. This was a new idea for the majority and when one compares the old ways with the new, and specifically focuses on the positive benefits, one can see why many people converted to Christianity.

To imagine that our bronze age and iron age ancestors were all devotedly spiritual and/or religious people is ludicrous. Why should they have been? It's true that the Church has held great power over people throughout its two thousand year reign but it hardly applies today. We live in a multicultural society with a glorious mix of belief systems, some based on ancient doctrines, and others loose and fluffy, with every conceivable faith in between. But we live in a time of economic power where material wealth has superseded its spiritual necessity.

Our relationship with the Green Man and his environment continues as always but in a nutshell the balance of need versus avarice is out of sync. We need to redress this balance quickly and simply by planting more trees than we cut. If, ideally, we planted three trees for every sacrificed member we will begin to address the problem. But contrary to modern thinking planting row upon row of pine soldiers may be sustainable but ecologically it is a potential disaster.

We need to replace the variety as well as the numbers.

So it seems to be mankind's interdependence with trees on all levels that is the ultimate definition of what the Green Man is about. What is he or she?

He is a wild and free untamed spirit. He is nature and man blended in perfect harmony. He offers new life and protection. He is the spring god calling to the young maidens (goddesses) to join him in the wild-wood. He is the thrust of spring growth, the product of the last season's union, fresh and green reaching upward towards the light of the Sun.

He is the Oak King of the summer solstice and the Holly King of the winter. He is the spirit of potential new life.

He is the archetype of the Fool in Tarot, wild and free and instinctive but full of potential.

There is one such example of a Green Man in St. Wandrille in Normandy that displays the characteristics of both Robin Hood and the Fool. He is Robin Hood, living the high life in the forest, trying to free the people from tyranny. So at home was he in his environment that he would seem to literally disappear from view when pursued. He has always been here and hopefully always will be. People from all walks of life and spiritual paths are interested in his message. He has become a green icon for the eco-warrior movement who actually risk sacrificing their lives to save individual trees.

People are in some part losing faith in science in spite of its obvious benefits and are worried about the downside to our advances and the damage we are inflicting upon nature. This is proof, I feel, that his message is undoubtedly being listened to. I also think that there is a strong desire to see more woodland returning and an even stronger one to protect what woodland we have left in this country by people from all walks of life. Luckily the spirit of the Green Man can touch all but the hardest of hearts, which is very evident if you ever find yourself involved in any road protests as he brings the most unlikely of people together in a common goal to save trees. So why do we have this great love for trees, even including the odd ancient gnarled stumpy oak resident on patches of green in city areas? Because we feel his fear, and like the fear wolves must have felt as they neared extinction we are aware of the reflection. As we destroy our landscape and cut down our old friends we are cutting our own limbs. By ridding ourselves of trees we deny ourselves the very air we breath and replace it with our own effluence that far exceeds nature's ability to absorb and transform. Our inner workings reflect from our environment and respect for individual trees is an example of this. Whilst I lived away from London a great battle commenced on my old backyard. This became the infamous Battle of George Green in Wanstead in northeast London. The battle to save several large chestnuts and many other trees and homes from the construction companies, paid by central government to build an extension to the M11, became national news. Eco-warriors descended from all over the country to chain themselves to the trees and live amongst the cranes and diggers. Local people from all walks of life and ages united to defend their heritage. For trees are our heritage and we hand them down, so great importance is placed upon them. This little-known corner of London fought hard and cost the road builders huge financial penalties. The road was built eventually and the landscape through Wanstonia (as it became known!) was sympathetically replaced but the same could not be said for the rest of the area it carved its way through. Friends and neighbours risked lives, arrest and even prison to prevent and restrict this intrusive 'growth' of arterial Britain.

The war continues to this day as each area is threatened so the legacy of places such as Twyford Down, Batheaston and Wanstead (to name but a few) increase the love and protection we feel collectively for our natural space. As each battle raises awareness greater emphasis is placed on conservation and retention of landscape and heritage. This in itself makes battles worth fighting in the name of the Green Man.

As children we grew up close to nature but many younger people today are not and to detach ourselves in this way is potentially harmful for both the Green Man and ourselves.

The virtual world of computer games may give their users a sense of God as they construct their simulated 'heavens and hells' but can they feel the weather upon their faces when playing? Not yet. Can they experience the delicious sensation of wet grass between their toes during a game? No. Do the more pleasant aromas of nature fill the air as they destroy yet another alien? Unlikely. But most importantly is there a force far more powerful than them inhabiting this world? No. Can they interact with this force at a magical level through these games? No. Nature still has far more to offer and is waiting patiently for them should the desire to really live occur to them at some point.

My generation didn't have these things and we made our own amusement. Although television had arrived it didn't absorb us to the extent modern youngsters are today by playing techno games. The world wasn't necessarily any safer than today with one exception, cars. The sheer volume of cars now lining and running up and down our streets makes them dangerous places for children to be out playing in. Media coverage of every fatal and near fatal accident doesn't help and a sense of overprotective paranoia has developed within certain groups of modern society. The park I grew up near is probably just as safe today as then but few children venture out without parents. Common sense and freedom have been sacrificed in favour of restriction and entertainment.

To exemplify this past/present misnomer many games were once attributed to the Green Man such as the practice of London children to select a Green Man who would hide in a pile of grass and then jump out when called by the others 'Green man, Green man, rise up and show yourself'. The hidden child would rise and chase the others amongst much shrieking and laughter. Whoever was caught became the Green Man and the end result was a lot of green children, I presume.

This brings me to another one of my local stories. This is of the Green children of Woolpit in Suffolk England known in earlier times as Wolfpit. At some time in the 12th century two children were found near one of the old wolf pits. They were of green skin and wearing a strange material. They spoke a different language and were adopted by the villagers but refused to eat anything except beans. The boy soon died but the girl survived and began to eat normal food and her skin became a normal colour.

Once she had learnt to speak English it is said she claimed she and her brother came from a strange twilight land on the other side of a broad river. They were tending their father's sheep and heard some bells, which they followed to a cavern. When they came out of their cavern they found themselves in the Wolfpits. She went on to live a long and happy life married in King's Lynn.

All aspects of our lives can be helped, improved, inspired and enriched by developing a deeper relationship with the Green Man. It is not necessary to select a specific tree to communicate with – just being out in the woods is enough – although you may well find yourself drawn to one particular type.

You can also connect with the Green Man at home but it is nice to have had some direct contact to draw upon for any workings or meditations.

Too many people these days are not getting out into nature enough and often this is due to the very hectic lives we all live but to attempt a connection with this spirit without any direct contact could well prove futile, I feel.

The spirit of the Green Man has so much to offer and all he asks is some attention and love in return. He transcends race and gender, he doesn't care what colour you are, how old you are, what language you speak, or what your preferred sexuality is. He is indifferent to these things. His divine love is unconditional and he will continue to bestow it upon us for as long as he survives. So it is on this basis that I totally believe that it was out of mutual respect rather than reverence that these faces were created.

Great love went into the carving and in some cases decorating of these faces. It would appear that although our early converts succumbed to the idea of Christ as a saviour of humanity the Green Man's image remained to remind us of our life-giving link with trees and eternal inter-dependence on them. We share fifty percent of our DNA with plant life. Now there's some food for thought.

Or as a quote from Horace says

Naturam expelles furca, tamen usque recurret

(You can drive out nature with a pitchfork, but she always returns.)

2

Making the Connection

So how do we make contact with him? That is the easiest thing to do. The essential spirit of the Green Man can be found in any woodland, particularly ancient woods.

Spending time out in the woods with an open heart, really feeling the energies of the trees, should get the connection going.

When I'm out alone or occasionally in company connecting with nature's energy three things 'happen'. I leave the rest of my world (as in 'leave your cares and worries behind for only then can you truly begin to open to the moment'). Once successfully disconnected from my everyday life I can begin to 'tune in' to the environment I'm now a part of. So to connect we must in effect be prepared to disconnect first.

The second phase is that of wonder and amazement of all that I see, hear, smell, touch and possibly taste so that I gradually 'attune' to the energy, which changes constantly.

The third phase is that of love and true opening of the heart towards all I am now very much in rhythm with and a part of.

It took some thought to break it down like this as the more time you spend doing this the less you consciously consider it and sooner or later 'it' just happens without any help.

How do you know if you have been successful? For each of us the experience is different. I hate to be enigmatic but suffice it to say you *will* know.

Some actually see *faces* appearing in the bark or leaves of the trees and may even experience many other 'strange' phenomena. You could be treated to a direct contact with some of the animals that live in the woods and find yourself face to face with a stag or owl. I have a friend who is so at home in this environment that birds just land on him unprovoked. As nature picks up on your love and gradually feels your energy as part of it, the response can be amazing. We were meant to live in harmony with each other but sadly most of nature these days just runs from our fear. Letting go of this fear can be hard for some who choose to harbour it but it is also the most liberating and loving thing we can do. Surrender the fear and open the heart then you too can release negativity and in so doing contribute towards world healing.

But in essence there is only one way to begin this process and that is to get outside into nature.

For many of you reading this book this is a regular practice and may even be your chosen way of life.

By choosing to work outside we connect with this spirit continuously. You may work in gardening, forestry or agriculture, for example. I chose to sacrifice a promising academic career and head for the depths of Epping Forest every day for ten hours of mucking out and riding. I don't regret it at all.

One should do these things when young so whether you want to travel the world on a moped or walk the length of Britain then do it, whilst you still can.

The spirit of the Green Man encourages us to follow our dreams with it in its environment. These are dreams of exploration and adventure they have an element of danger and are leading us down paths filled with alive moments and crystal clarity.

There will be times of much and times of little, times of beauty and times of death, times of frustration and times of achievement. All times are possible within this spirit.

To begin your journey start by looking out of the nearest window from which you can see a tree. Now just sit and relax. Focus on the tree.

Look down as far as you can towards its roots then allow your eyes to draw as slowly as you want up its trunk to its branches.

Notice everything about it, everything. Study it in detail. Really get to know this tree.

Watch its branches respond to the wind. Let your eyes gently follow its movement without deliberately moving them.

Feel the energy of this movement.

Now feel love for this tree, if needed relate the love to actual feelings you have of loving another. Feel the love return.

Focus on your tree as often as possible for as long as you reasonably can.

The more often you do this the more internal peace you should feel.

This is the beginning.

You may now feel the need to explore farther afield but start from your chosen tree and work out. By getting to know your immediate environment you are making a definite connection with the space you currently occupy.

This can have a profound effect on your psyche and will intensify your desire to understand the spirit and mix with it at every possible opportunity.

My local relationship with this energy drives me on when things get bad and living in close proximity to two local high schools gives me endless litter to pick up on behalf of this venerable spirit. Joy. As I mentioned earlier there is always dark as well as light and litter is one such dark. We all have bugbears and litter is mine, I find it offensive and an insult to our natural spaces not to mention a potential toxic hazard to wildlife and ourselves!

Once you feel a positive benefit from your tree-gazing days it's time for a more serious relationship to develop.

If possible set aside a whole day to sit in a quiet place amongst some trees.

The season must be taken into account so dress accordingly. The magic of each season varies considerably and so will particular days and moon phases.

For the majority of people I would recommend spring, summer and autumn to be the most comfortable months but don't be put off by winter – just be prepared.

A whole day might be too much for you to start with so you can always begin with a dawn to mid-day stint the first time and mid-day to sunset the next time.

I would try to arrive just before dawn, taking a small packed lunch and some water for the day ahead.

(I don't recommend taking the family dog, as dogs can get pretty bored, are a constant distraction, and can put off any wildlife from coming near you.)

Find a comfortable position facing the east and relax.

Start by closing your eyes and concentrate on the smells you detect.

Take normal regular breaths but spend a few minutes doing this.

Now open your eyes slowly and allow ten minutes or so for them to adjust to the new light.

While you await dawn's arrival focus on any noises you can hear for a few minutes.

As dawn begins just sit and enjoy every single visual minute of its rising.

Notice how the light of the environment changes as it rises and the shadows grow longer.

After a while (I have no idea when this will be as each of us is different) you may begin to feel uncomfortable. Try to ignore this and focus inwardly upon your breathing for a few minutes. Keep your mind focused on inhaling and exhaling. Don't be irritated if your mind tries to wander. Stay at peace with yourself and focus back on your breathing.

Once you feel the wave of discomfort pass allow yourself to take notice of your space again.

Now it is time to focus on one particular spot. It can be what ever you feel drawn to. Don't be put off if it is a dark sight that draws the eye. There may be a very valid reason for you to stare death and decay in the face.

Whatever it is that attracts you focus on it intently for as long as you can.

During these times great insights are often discovered both on a personal level and a wider one.

Some people experience a whole gambit of emotions when sitting in nature for a day.

By mid morning you will probably need to go to the loo and eat so go ahead and do it.

I will warn against eating too much, though. The fuller our stomachs are the less of a spiritual connection we are able to feel.

Now it is time slowly, and I mean slowly, to explore your chosen place of contemplation.

Spend a couple of hours really looking at all you can see remembering to use all your senses and stay mindful of them. Indulge in some tactile exploration but don't feel limited in just using your hands. If the urge to rub hazel leaves over your face comes upon you then go for it. You might feel the desire to dance but bear in mind if part of your journey is to draw wildlife to you throughout your day loud stomping will clear a wide radius of such opportunities.

Don't get me wrong. I'm all in favour of a quick surreptitious swirl but I prefer my days to be as still as possible.

I like to spend the afternoon in one of three ways: I will write, draw or sleep normally.

Sleeping in nature is definitely to be encouraged. Your dreams will be full of magic if you are really lucky.

You can do whatever you feel like doing with your afternoon but be prepared to return to your original point of tranquillity just before sunset.

Once the sun begins its descent turn and face it in meditation of your space again until its last rays disappear over the horizon.

By now you should be ravenous and full of energy, inspiration, wisdom, but with an inner sense of peace.

Even doing this once in your lifetime will have a profound effect on your life.

I think everyone should watch the sun rise and set all in one day at least once in their lives.

Now a connection should have been made and you are poised on the edge of a great adventure if you want it.

After a while, and I have no idea how long it will take, you may notice you are drawn to certain types of tree or a specific one. At this point I would recommend you acquire a notebook to record your findings. Make note of the type of tree and its location. Start to see it in relationship with its immediate environment. Make note of any insights or inspirations that occur whilst in communion with its spirit.

You may feel a creative burst and a need to express it in some way such as prose, song or art. Your results may astound you.

Your relationship with trees will be unique to you on all levels and the love that can be shared between you will be special to you also. But don't be surprised if you're facing dark thoughts or occasionally hit with fear or desperation. This spirit contains all our joint experiences, man and tree together. Don't make the mistake of thinking this is a fluffy violet fairy of tambourine waving and romantic poetry. It can be, but that is only one aspect of it and it has many others.

> *The humble goose herder trudges alone, his pockets bulging with*
> *silver,*
> *Back to his home on the other side of the great forest.*
> *Rain begins to fall and darkness surrounds him.*
> *The wind drives mercilessly into his face.*
> *His head down, he tries to stay on the narrow muddy path ahead.*
> *Lightning strikes a tree in his path and a branch falls down upon*
> *his*
> *Wet and wretched body.*
> *As he lies on his back dying crushed by the weight of the huge*
> *branch he looks up at the black scorched scar of the tree above.*
> *They die together.*
> *Man and tree.*
> *In life and in death.*
> *Joined for eternity.*

This story came to me in meditation and served to reveal a part of our journey together. We are bound to one another eternally, always have been and always will be. Try meditating on an imaginary life devoid of trees and see how far you get. Not far I'll wager.

Now try the opposite and look outwardly around you, now, yes now, and count how many trees you can see in your home.

Lost count yet?

I've just spun round on my office chair and counted evidence of at least twelve individuals and that was without counting the various mounds of paper bestrewn about my desk.

So is the Green Man simply the spirit of all trees or does it encompass all green life? Yes and no.

The important fact to digest about our interpretation of it is that we have personified it.

Most images and myths pertaining to this spirit admittedly are male and many people will claim this is a purely male entity, but I disagree. I see it as androgynous.

By giving any spiritual energy physical attributes and then naming it we influence our perception of it.

As I mentioned earlier we find the Green Man linked throughout history with deities such as Dionysus, Silvanus, Pan, Herne the Hunter, Cernunnos, and I feel Diana, to name but a few and they all have one common denominator, nature as in trees or leaves.

For our ancestors, personification made perfect sense so they gave most of the energies they came across human characteristics or blended them with what they perceived as their own wyrd.

The Green Man, or his equivalent, was harder to pin down. When working with and identifying with the more commonly known energies of his manifestation, such as Cernunnos for example, one feels the excited call of new spring growth comparable to the energy experienced during human adolescence. When sitting quietly in one of my favourite spots I feel balance and harmony and an inextricable link leading to a holistic world of pure magic.

Therein for my own part lies the difference, or one of them.

Looking back a few thousand years it is reasonable to assume that the 'faces' often visible in the bark of some trees were the conception of this personification. Our ancestors would have recognised this as a special sign or connection with them. Considering many of them living in northern Europe, where most of the images occur, almost certainly lived in or near woodland it makes sense that this was an instant and direct form of recognition. So do trees grow faces deliberately or did the belief that they did suffice? This chicken and egg situation is unlikely ever to be resolved and I also feel is irrelevant nowadays.

Over thousands of millennia the spirit has grown and our relationship with this spirit has changed dramatically. It is foolhardy and probably inaccurate to believe that all the ancestors revered nature and only took from it what they needed. With so much in the Garden of Eden some wastage was bound to occur.

I don't believe this was a problem but the ancestors had some pretty screwed up ways of relating to nature's spirit and their other gods and goddesses, human sacrifice being one of them. I find it hard to believe that the Green Man asked for such cruelty to occur even if for the people of some cultures it was seen as an honour.

Nature, I believe, sees death as an incidental necessity but still senses the loss.

Trees may suffocate each other out and inadvertently lay down their life for the sake of another but not without fighting for as much life as they can get first. Its not a voluntary act, just nature responding to its environment.

I believe human sacrifices were deemed necessary by human invention or reflection, not by any higher wisdom learnt from nature. Sacrifice in life is unavoidable so we should be thoughtful, ethical and moral in our present day execution of this rite. Whether we are at one extreme forced to relinquish a loved one or suffer loss in any way it is all a form of sacrifice. Like many practising pagans today I often give offerings to the woods, rivers and wells I visit and they vary from the purely symbolic, as in a protection ritual, to the more personal sacrifice of giving up something of sentimental or special value when asking for a magical boost to one's endeavours. I was taught that it operates on a sliding scale but also am wise enough now to know that if I harbour any doubt or negativity from my request it is less likely to manifest or may do so in a form not previously considered. One has to feel right about these acts before committing to them.

As an example I heard of a young man who longed for his first love and spent many an hour communing with nature, inspired with romantic notions but only in a dreamy way. One day his request was answered and at long last a girl came into his life and they spent many a happy hour together walking amid the bluebells.

But the young man had only concentrated on the light and fluffy side of his love and refused to acknowledge everyday reality. Not long after choosing to live together they were tested by external disruptive influences and without boring you with the sordid details their relationship became hard work for both of them. He couldn't cope with the everyday down to earth stresses of life, especially the financial one. She in turn resented his attitude towards the money and therein lay the problems.

It was interesting to note that during the last few weeks the couple hardly spent any time together in nature. As they turned from the magic that joined them so the spell was broken.

MEDITATION

For some of you reading this book meditating is already a well established part of your lives but for those of you unfamiliar with such practices we are going to look at how it can deepen your connection with the Green Man. The methods I have chosen are some that I use and have found helpful in understanding his message. Some of the questions I have posed have been general or global and others for my immediate environment. He can also help considerably in accessing the dormant parts of our psyche and opening them up for us to see ourselves in a more open and clear way.

Our personal inner world is unique to each of us in many respects but also holds a key to deeper understanding of the Green Man.

So what is meditation, why do it, and how?

Well, according to the dictionary meditation is 'to reflect deeply especially on spiritual matters'. So following this concept it follows that we all meditate in some form or another throughout our lives whether consciously or not.

Why do we do this? Well, because it is within our nature to question everything and try to understand it. This understanding raises our levels of personal awareness and increases our sensitivity to our environment. Or to put it more simply we fine-tune ourselves.

Is it integral to the Green Man and paganism in general? I think it is but some may disagree. Contrary to popular misconceptions meditation doesn't have to be a conscious act but can happen inadvertently and the most active form of meditation we ALL indulge in on a daily basis is daydreaming. This is your mind at its most fantastical (albeit dark sometimes) and magical.

Popular myths

'I can't meditate, I've tried everything'

The key word is 'trying'. Stop trying and relax; let your mind flow and eventually you will be deeply meditating or asleep!

'I thought you had to empty your mind'

There are forms of meditation that 'still' the mind but it is never 'empty'. To still the mind we focus upon one thing whether it be our breathing or an object or the flow of energy into our chakras. It all helps with much practice to 'still and calm' the mind.

'I've tried everything. I can't do it'

What are you trying to do and why try? The conscious mind can feel like an enemy to meditation but it isn't. You simply haven't found a way to suit your particular wiring yet; bet you daydream lots though! Many a daydream or introspective moment leads to increased clarity and eureka moments so don't worry – you probably do it more than most naturally and just didn't realise!

'I can't raise energy'

Rubbish! We are all energetic beings just wired differently. Without energy you would cease to exist so you raise it constantly, but I under-stand that the energy of the body and mind is not your objective and spiritual energy is required. One of the most common blocks to raising this energy is fear of letting go or surrendering which is why we place ourselves within protective spheres. Our ancestors may or may not have done this but we do as it works for us. Once we feel safe we can relax and open up to the pure energy of spirit. (This doesn't include deliberate invocations.) Love is the purest form of spiritual energy and by focusing upon anything we feel love for we allow spiritual energy to flow. See, you *can* do it.

'My mind always wanders'

So does everyone's – you are not alone. During long meditations Buddhist monks are hit with sticks to stop them wandering or falling asleep! Imagine you are riding a horse or driving a car and the steering is challenged: this is the mind wandering. Just pull it back to where you want it to be. Keep this up long enough and over a period of time it wanders less. This can take time and patience though. Forgive yourself. Relax.

'I've tried for hours and it keeps going wrong'

Don't 'try' and definitely keep it short to begin with but remember there is no 'wrong'. Short regular sessions are best.

MY TIPS

- Keep it brief to begin with
- Choose a quiet time and place
- Preparation: relaxing bath or invigorating shower
- Use aids: incense, candles, crystals, wood, flowers, etc., whatever works for you
- Avoid a full tummy: do it before eating
- Ground yourself afterwards: eat, drink, jump about

There are many forms of meditation and many varied reasons for partaking of it. The three forms we are going to touch upon are

1. Relaxation
2. Raising energy
3. Trance

RELAXATION

To begin we need to relax. Relaxing in the Green Man's environment should be relatively simple if you choose your spots for their comfort as well as their magical essence.

In order to become proficient in your meditation you need to learn how to relax and for some of us this is easier than for others. *In the beginning there was the breath.* Breathing is something we all take for granted but to actually focus upon our breathing is unusual and yet natural. We are all a part of the universal breath and need to connect with this in order to relax. First we need to relax the body and in order to achieve this one must be comfortable. Being comfortable takes many forms and if it is your wish to use relaxation techniques to aid restful sleep then lay down. If you wish to remain awake then assume whatever position is most relaxing for you. Contrary to popular belief we do not have to adopt a 'lotus' stance – any position is fine that allows you to inhale and exhale fully. So don't squash your lungs.

We are vain here in the west and spend far too much time breathing from the top of our lungs, as to breath from lower would mean letting go of our stomach muscles and let it all hang out. Let it all hang out.

To begin we will take a few cleansing breaths and clear any stale air from the bottom of our lungs. These need to be long slow deep ones about half a dozen should do it. Don't worry if you cough – it's all a part of the cleansing process.

Now to relax your breathing you should just breathe normally and focus on your solar plexus. If your mind wanders don't worry. Just bring it back to your breath. Doing this for a few minutes each day will calm and centre your spiritual self.

If you are very tense beforehand try tensing and relaxing all your main muscle groups in turn, starting at the bottom and working your way up; or have a soak in the tub; or if you are really lucky get someone to massage you!

It is very important not to rush this: work at your own pace. If thoughts come in don't follow them, just focus back on your breath, let them pass like little fluffy clouds in a clear blue sky.

Candle relaxation is another popular form of meditation and is simply done by lighting a candle (white is best) and use the breathing technique whilst focusing on the flame.

Remember your only aim should be to relax, nothing more, nothing less.

RAISING ENERGY

Drawing on the energy of the Green Man is so easy as it is all around us. By deliberately getting out into his space and finding a sacred spot to experience your deeper relationship you can start to really feel the magic of his force. This form of meditation is to my mind intrinsic to any magical working and therefore a useful skill to learn. But even if your wish is purely to gain personal strength, of the inner variety, then this will still help. We are going to try to draw ethereal energy into us and then direct it in a deliberate manner. Raising this energy is often a skill most pagans have difficulty with but I personally think it helps to focus one's intent and without the 'magic' the results are often weaker. This can take time to master. It took me over a year of daily practice to become moderately useful but for others it simply flows naturally. Don't worry or panic. It will happen eventually if you persevere.

There are several ways in which we can do this and we are going to try two methods in the hope that one will suit you.

The first method includes a certain level of visualisation but don't worry about it, just feel if you can't see.

Either standing or sitting we are going to imagine each one of us is a tree. Starting at our feet we are going to 'see' roots growing out of them and reaching down deep into the ground. Feel the earth beneath your feet as these roots slowly feel their way into it.

Spread them out round any obstacles deeper into the ground until you feel the energy of the Green Man start to pulsate up into them. Take a second to feel love for the earth beneath you and let this love draw up the roots into your feet and legs. Let this energy flow upwards into your body, up your spine, filling you with love for the miracle of life. As the energy reaches your arms, release it out into the air so it fills us all with its spirit.

Above us is the sun. Let its light flow down upon your branches filling you with its love and invigorating your skin with its touch.

Now you are at peace, rooted yet free to be yourself.

Enjoy this moment before drawing the energy back down into the ground from whence it came.

Thank the Green Man for his generosity inwardly or outwardly.

Questions that might be personally relevant

- Did you have any feelings as to what tree you actually were?
- Does that mean anything to you?
- Do you feel energised?

This method is best employed outside but also works indoors. By raising Earth energy we stay grounded but vitalised just as a tree does as it receives nourishment from the soil. The tops of our bodies receive this energy and it interacts with light energy causing a general feeling of good will and flowing love throughout.

The second method we will try is Hindu in origin and my preferred method. This is chakra activation.

Many of the methods of meditation we use today are Hindu in origin and chakras are no exception. They may not have any direct relevance to our indigenous ancestors but they work and for that reason alone I use them.

Chakras are energy points throughout our bodies that more or less link up with certain glands in our bodies. These glands are responsible for maintaining our equilibrium and by focusing upon them we can strengthen ourselves on all levels. We have seven basic chakras.

- Our root chakra is the base of our now defunct tail or coccyx and relates to our earthly survival matters. Its colour is red. Buddhists see them as flowers opening but I prefer to see them as spinning balls of light. Use whatever method works best.
- The next chakra is the sacral or genital area and relates to sex and reproduction. Its colour is orange.

- The third chakra is our belly and focuses around your solar plexus. It relates to your digestive and emotional well being and its colour is yellow.
- The forth chakra is your heart and relates to loving and giving. It is green.
- Next we have the throat chakra connected to breathing and communicating. Its colour is blue.
- Now we get to the third eye chakra, just above and between your eyebrows. Its colour is purple and will buzz (no, not audibly – it's more of a sensation) when activated. This is your psychic eye.
- Last, for our purposes, as there are more, we come to the crown chakra which is your mind and is white. As this one 'opens' you can draw down light energy from above with each exhalation. This can manifest itself as spiralling energy flowing up and down your spine and can feel ecstatic. Some people like to spin this energy outside the body in two circles around their aura or natural energy field.

To do a chakra meditation we must first get comfy, relax, then start to visualise each one in turn activating as spinning lights within our body from base upwards, drawing the energy of each into the next until you are buzzing with spiritual light up and down your body.

To do this takes much time and patience, but is well worth it. Don't rush it. If one chakra needs more time to get going then give it more attention. I prefer to draw energy up with each inhalation and spin with each exhalation. Believe me, this gives your mind more than enough to concentrate on so wandering can be less of a problem.

Once you master activating chakras you will often find you experience some of your most profound meditations.

When you have had enough or finish (time taken is up to you) then you need to close them down afterwards. Start at the top and work down, turning each one off like a light switch as you go.

Chakra activation is great for many things such as the following.

- Cleansing spiritually.
- Energy raising for magical workings. You direct the energy into your magical tools, or directly to goal through your hands and state your intent, pointing if required towards the relevant direction.
- Healing with pure energy is a great cleanser and will clear out any mental, physical and spiritual blockages. But be warned: this can feel quite overpowering at times so don't be surprised at any reaction you get. Just relax.

- Calming the mind and aiding better concentration your wakefulness should become more alert and learning can be less problematic.
- De-stressing. It's a brilliant way of calming down and ridding yourself of pain or negativity.

The list could go on.

WARNING

Leaving your chakras open leaves you vulnerable to soaking up everybody else's 'stuff' and this in turn can make you ill or negative depending on what you absorb.

If worried protect yourself beforehand.

I've accidentally left my third eye open many times after Tarot readings and had some quite horrendous headaches so watch out and try not to forget to close them.

If you do forget and leave one or more open just close and meditate again fairly soon to clear you of any unwanted attachments.

By combining the tree root method with this method some astounding results can occur! It is quite possible to meet a personification of the Green Man this way as he is very much alive and well, just waiting for us to peek into his world and say hello.

I personally try to do it at least once a week now, but to begin with I did it every day for a year! Some dedication you may think. Not really. I was determined and had few distractions so could afford the time.

Some people find they have more luck raising energy through dance and/or chanting, which is fine, but as I am not a practitioner of these crafts I can't teach that which I know little about experientially.

The basic premise of dance is well known as a method of raising energy and is probably one of our oldest root practices. My mum uses it by simply preparing herself first and just going into what I describe as ecstatic free fall. Go for it if you wish. There are no rules and its very effective but tiring. Morris dancers would probably agree!

Chanting is different, and it is well known among many ancient traditions that chanting has a profound effect upon us. To repetitively chant a sound such as OM or a word or short verse keeps the mind busy and focused whilst the body may feel an instinctive desire to rock gently. This form of meditation is very relaxing and calming but holding it for long periods produces more intense effects such as visualisations, altered states, journeys on the astral plane and literal out-of-body experiences. Powerful stuff!

TRANCE

All trance work is rooted deeply in our shamanic past and has been used for a wide variety of purposes over thousands of years. It isn't necessary to have a specific purpose to your trance work as much can come out of spontaneous moments. This method can work well for those wishing to advance towards astral projection and actually visualise our friend the Green Man in three dimensions.

Trance work is used frequently for a variety of reasons. Some use it for shamanic purposes, some for deeper insight, and some to raise psychic levels of sensitivity.

Hindu breathing method

We are going to take our breathing practice a step further and use one of the many Hindu breathing methods to induce trance states.

By a process of clearing, relaxing and timing we will move into trance, hopefully.

The timing involves deliberate breathing, so breathe in for a count of six and out for three. This timing can be done with varied amounts but 8/4, 6/3 or 4/2 seems to be easiest in my experience. Like all meditation it takes practice so don't panic if you find it tricky to start. Some people are very susceptible to this form of breathing and can trance out quite quickly. Just come back to normal at any time. Remember you hold the reins of meditation and the horse should always stop if pulled hard enough. If you do panic and can't break the pattern or find yourself hyperventilating, just jerk a part of your body and you should come back to earth. You may get a bump though! During this form of meditation it is best just to let images, smells, sounds, feelings etc. flow. Just watch objectively. Many a wise word comes out of such experiences. Having a steady rhythm of drum or metronome can help with this one.

GROUNDING PATH WORKING

Path workings seem to be flavour of the month at all workshops and some moots these days, but why do we do them? Are we curious about the inner workings of our minds or are we hoping for answers? Both probably.

Path workings are simply guided meditations where the mind can naturally be led where the path worker takes them. For this reason they have simple rules. The first is that of creating the scene or starting point. It may involve a doorway or tunnel but a barrier of some type has to be crossed. They then enter a magical world where they are invited to interact with all sorts of things from deities to fluffy bunnies, depending on the subject matter or essence of the working. Then it is seen as imperative that the route taken is repeated in reverse to extract you safely from the magical realms of your mind (and frequently the minds of others) to your normal grounded personal space.

This type of meditation in the wrong hands can be a dangerous tool so it is important that you understand the concept and reason for the working before joining in. You may not always feel in the right space to do a path working, and if so then don't, and don't feel pressurised. No one will care or notice if you just sit quietly reading whilst all around slip off as it were.

When creating your own path working, take time and visualise it yourself or better still use a real place. Keep it fairly simple but don't rush – everyone needs a chance to keep up so take time and have decent pauses between each change within the journey.

The following path working is one I've used to ground people after meditation workshops.

It is sunset on a cool autumn evening and we are standing on the edge of a great pine forest. Ahead of us is a flat, wide, straight track that disappears into the trees.

(Pause)

The air is still and quiet as we walk forwards together up the ride. As we all walk along we notice animals darting almost invisibly in the dappled light through the dark woods and hear the rooks caw as they land in tree tops around us.

(Pause)

Soon we see a gap in the trees up ahead to the left and turn into it following a deer track down between the grass and thistles. We reach a fence and turn with the path to the right down a steep bank. The short twisty lichen-covered trees give off a slightly musty smell as we follow along down to the bottom.

(Pause)

We reach a small brook that crosses our path and to our right a natural amphitheatre reveals itself with a round pool in its centre, the source of our stream. Reeds and other plants grow tall and proud and a lone hawthorn grows on its bank. Under the tree a spring of pure water bubbles forth from deep under ground.

We sit here a bit enjoying the peace and tranquillity, smelling, watching, listening and touching our natural space.

(Wait a few minutes)

Now the shadows lengthen and the air grows cooler so reluctantly we get up to leave with love this place behind before it gets dark.

Walking back up the steep bank we hear the early call of an owl in the distance and push on up to the top.

(Pause)

Carefully we pick our way back along the stubbly grass until we reach the wide track. As we walk along the track we sense something behind us and stop all turning to see what it is that demands our attention.

(Pause)

(*This is the path worker inviting you to 'ken or see'. You will all see whatever is personal to you unless the person talking has projected an image for you to pick up. I placed a small grey female wolf on this spot last time and several people saw her. This can be an awakening moment for people.*)

Once seen we return to walking and enjoy the last few yards of our journey home to where we set off.

This path-working helps us to connect astrally in his environment and it can help introduce the concepts without being to intense.

GREEN MAN PATH-WORKING

This can be learnt for individual meditation or read out to a friend or group as a guided working.

It is an early May morning and we stand in a field on the edge of an ancient coppice woodland. Ahead of us is a narrow earth path leading into the woods. The sun beats down on us and the air is full of bird song. The leaves of the hazel, oak, ash, blackthorn and alder are fresh and green vibrant with new life. Each of us holds a small offering for the spirit of the Green Man.

(Pause)

We all walk forward smelling wafts of wild honeysuckle that grows tenaciously around the young hazel. Either side of us the trees are buzzing with youthful exuberance as butterflies flutter and deer tread lightly in the copse enjoying the odd new bud. Soon we reach a gap in the trees on our right.

(Pause)

We follow the path through the carpet of bluebells to a small clearing. Bracken grows all around the edge, framing the more mature oaks and birch. One solitary twisty small birch tree occupies the centre of this glade with a tall straight oak behind it. We stop here a while.

(Longer pause)

Soon a stag appears from behind the oak. He is huge, far larger than any you've seen before but not so big as to seem ridiculous. He stands firm, his eyes fixed on ours, his magnificent antlers held proudly aloft, his thick soft mane hiding the strong muscles of his neck, and his legs stand square. He commands our attention and yet as we look deeply within his eyes we see them change. Now his face takes on human features and we see the young man within. He circles us slowly, allowing us to smell the scent of the beast and feel his heat as steam coming off his coat. Now he walks back towards our tree and disappears behind it.

(Pause)

We stay looking at the magnificent oak, its rutted bark, its branches reaching up for light, its bright new green leaves – and as we do this a face appears from the tree. The eyes of a deer, the nose of a man and the lips of a woman with leaves growing out of its ears and scalp. The face emerges from the tree slowly with skin as green as winter moss.

(Pause)

For each of us the Green Man/Lady has arrived and a magical mist now surrounds the clearing. As we each face this face we face ourselves.

Now is the time for personal communication. Speak to your face and see what it has to tell you.

(Leave a few minutes for this)

Before we leave we all place our offerings around the twisty birch.

52

As each of us has had communion, now is the time to leave. We bid farewell to our friend and return back to the path.

The mist lifts and sunlight shines down strongly through the thick branches, faerie folk dart here and there, little bells can be heard tinkling and the smell of wild garlic fills the air.

(Pause)

Energised by our meeting we skip and hop playfully back to the main path and turning left make our way happily towards the edge of the woods again.

It is important to check everyone is OK afterwards, and having something to eat and drink to help ground them is also a good idea.

The interaction is very personal and it is important to decide in advance whether you want to talk about this afterwards or not.

Sometimes people get stuck at a certain point on path-workings and others can even get lost, so reassure everyone that they can always just wait for the others to catch up with them if they wish.

'If the power to think is a remarkable gift, then the power to not think is even more so'

Sri Aurobindo
Hindu Sage

'Our future is our present from the past'

Anon (OK, it was me, but I could have subconsciously got it from elsewhere. Who knows, but it's an example of what can come through in clear moments or when fishing!)

SEASONAL GREEN MAN CONNECTIONS

Once your connection strengthens you may feel the need to visit your sacred spaces on specific days throughout the year.

A spring connection

If it occurs to you that you would like to welcome and honour the arrival of the Green Man in spring in a sacred and significant way then these are simply ideas for you to ponder, nothing more, nothing less.

To truly identify a specific day to celebrate any season is difficult which is why we have designated days for such rituals. This isn't necessary at all and you might feel strongly that another day is more appropriate for many reasons. It doesn't matter.

So whether you decide to recognise Imbolc/Candlemas, the spring equinox or any day between those dates it's very much up to you. The moon phase may be relevant if planning to hold a night-time ritual or welcome the first moon of spring. I personally prefer to set aside a dawn for such activities and lay much trust in my sense of smell when determining the day itself. Each season does seem to be marked by a changed aroma, but this is personal and may not resonate with you. Again, it doesn't matter.

As you may have noticed the word 'ritual' has crept in and I wish to be clear about this. A ritual is something we deliberately decide to do that holds spiritual and/or special significance to us, but having said that there are those who would consider picking up dog mess in the garden on a regular basis a ritual. Rituals are acts we repeat and consider sacred whilst doing them. So basically anything can be ritualistic, from washing up to planting seeds – it just depends on the emphasis behind it. As I am a spontaneous type I like to let the spirit of the Green Man decide what it wants from me rather than sticking to a particular set plan for each changing season. You could be different and prefer the idea of always following the same pattern. It really isn't important, as it is more about whether you do it and what you do than the method employed.

If the intent is pure and from the heart all will be well.

Talking of wells, these are traditionally dressed in spring to mark the melting of winter and fresh flowing new life giving waters from the earth, so visiting a local well is one good way in which to mark spring. Some believe this is a direct form of contact with the essence of the Green Lady, or in other words the energy is strongly feminine. There are two wells near me and I like to visit them fairly frequently, taking an offering and spending some quality time opening up to the energy of these places. If the water is running clear and high I sometimes collect some for later use. I like to put a few drops in my animals' drinking water as I totally believe it helps, and if my sixteen-year-old dog is anything to go by then it does!

The offering can be anything you like so long as it isn't going to pollute or harm the well in anyway. The time you spend there and what you do whilst there is very much up to you and anything from meditating quietly to calling on the spirit of the well to wish you luck is all equally valid.

54

Another way to welcome the spirit of the Green Man in spring is to simply go outside on the day you have chosen and just take a good hard look at nature beginning to bud and 'tune in' to the new energy as it rises from deep underground. Just simply walking in a natural or quiet spot will lift your spirits and fill you with hope for the season ahead. This is also the sowing season so planting some seeds and nurturing them is also a good way to welcome spring, but I'd advise you to do it only if you really want that which you sow. I have friends who prefer to get together and specifically hold a group ritual to welcome each season as it helps keep them focused and the combined energies help strengthen each of their individual expectations of the coming season. They simply set an outdoor altar/table and dress it with early snowdrops or similar and have a representation of each element on it whilst each in turn reads something significant to them personally that they have all agreed to beforehand. This deliberate act gives them great joy and satisfaction on a deep and spiritual level so if you have friends you really love and trust a seasonal get together can be most fulfilling.

You don't have to be pagan or follow any particular path at all to enjoy and welcome the spirit of the spring Green Man into your heart. We are all children of nature and as such will respond to its changes whilst acknowledging the divine miracle of life as we so do.

Summer connection

Traditionally the 1st of May/Beltane or thereabouts signifies the start of the summer season and as we have discovered is very much a time associated with the energy of the Green Man at his most fertile. This is the growing time and nature's energy is at its most obvious and forceful now.

Summer has its own unique rhythm that explodes into being and then mellows subtly as the weeks go on. There are many ways to connect with the Green Man at this time and for me it involves spending as much time out in the woods as possible just to enjoy quality time alone in his presence. The magic of early summer is an energy we can all tap into and are usually aware of. The vibrant fresh new green leaves buzz with pure life, invigorating us as we feel the sap begin to rise. This energy is most creative and can manifest itself in several ways, from being inspired to write, paint, dance or sing to a general desire to 'do more', as it were. Sexually we are also at our most stimulated now and for some this might be welcomed but for others it can be problematic, so for those of you single folk affected by this seasonal frustration my

55

advice is this: use the energy in another way, i.e. direct it creatively somehow.

Traditionally we can celebrate the start of summer by visiting his environment and also any ecologically biased work will be much appreciated now by the Green Man. You might like to attend a specific ritual in your area by supporting the local morris side or joining in with any of the many Beltane celebrations around the country. We can give thanks for the return of the sun and its life-giving properties by holding a group celebration, even if all this amounts to is a picnic in his environment; as long as the love for the space is true, you are taking part in his season. For me this time of year is about getting on with life and making the most of the light now available from gardening to long summer walks by twinkling rivers. It's all a part of the season and is often the time I feel at my most invigorated and positive. Its also the time we often take a holiday somewhere special and this year we spent a wonderful week down in southern Cornwall enjoying the Green Man's influence amongst the beautiful gardens and secluded coves. Late summer encourages us all to lengthen our days and be out as much as possible rather than sitting in watching our TVs, so responding to the spirit of the Green Man's cycles can change us for the better it seems. Nature's energy is free and readily available for all – it's just a case of getting out there and soaking it up with love and respect for the product of the previous season. This is also the season of the oak as king of the forest, presiding over his woodland in quiet authority. Oaks are very special to us in this country and most of us have an affinity with them. I have several oak friends whom I visit at this time of year and usually just by sitting with them answers flow, energy rises and after time spent with them I am ready for whatever I wish to achieve, enriched by their timeless sense and wisdom. This is also the best time for fertility rituals and much success can be had by direct experiential access to his world with your loving partner, especially if you want a child.

Autumn connection

Now the nights are drawing in and an evening chill is in the air: autumn has arrived. The leaves are just starting to turn and harvests are being gathered. As we feel this gradual slowing down it's time to take stock of the achievements of the year past. The Green Man energy is visually surreal at this time, challenging our perceptions before it gradually settles back down for winter. The ground is covered in an array of colours from green to yellow to brown and deep rich reds reminding me that our own autumn years can be as beautiful as this if we let them. He appears a little older and wiser but still full of creative surprises during this time.

Were your winter worries founded? Did spring fill you with hope and energy? Has summer been fulfilling? These are just some of the thoughts that can flow at this time.

Again it might be hard to give a definitive day or date to the start of this season but for most of us in this hemisphere it starts in September or thereabouts. The 21st represents the equinox or when days and nights are of equal length, and as this equal tension manifests so stress levels can rise as we dash about doing all those jobs we should have done earlier whilst enjoying summer. The annual leaf clearing itself can be fun though, and making this part of your autumn ritual is a good idea. As you sweep away the dead and dying leaves give thanks inwardly or outwardly for the wonderful colours and life now spent. Traditionally it's time to prepare for the winter ahead from repairing one's home (if needed) to stocking up on edible summer goodies like apples or making preserves. As we save that which we can from nature's bounty, so nature itself retreats underground to a warmer safer place. The energy can still be felt but its rhythm is different, lower, as the earth itself pulls the sap below. Harvest festivals are held and thanks are given for the season of growth, for it is this growth we all rely upon and in this time of super-markets and general detachment its easy to forget these things. Children are encouraged to bring along food to schools for local charities and good causes, so it is a time of giving and sharing, helping us to remember that we must be prepared to share in order to survive. You never know when at some point in the future you might benefit from such generosity of spirit, so its good to give.

As we enter this seasonal tide we shift from the fiery summer months to the more light and airy tide. This is a time for thought and reflection and as we draw nearer to the end of October it's time for the veil between life and death to thin. Many a ghost of Green Men past can manifest at this time and it is normal for us to feel dreamy and lacking physical incentive for a while. But mentally and spiritually we can be most stimulated even if our bodies require we slow down. At this time we remember our ancestors, so visiting them is a pretty good way of connecting with the magical energy. Again it is most likely to be in the Green Man's environment, as I have yet to visit a churchyard or crematorium that doesn't have trees. These watchers over the dead are our link with the past and as such can, if you are open to it, give direct access if required. Don't be scared, for I totally believe we all have far more to fear from the living than the dead.

Walks in woodland can be pretty spectacular throughout this season. With the amazing variety of colours on show it's almost as if he is saying 'How's this for a finale?'. So again I stress get out there and make time to visit his space; don't miss out on this yearly event. It's well worth it. The most spectacular shows of autumn are usually in arboretums and many exist in this country. Westonbirt in Gloucestershire is probably the best I've seen to date, although there are many others.

Winter connection

By December winter is usually pretty set in and we all having to contend with shorter days and less light. Most of our trees are now bare and create magnificent living sculptures standing stark in the landscape. Appearing dead, they hibernate as do many of our woodland creatures, and we also feel the need to sleep a little more than normal.

The spirit of the Green Man is still there, vibrant in our evergreens, protective and reassuring. This energy is traditionally thought of as crone but the wise old Green Man links with her, caring for her underground like a benevolent grandfather.

Our artificial lights stimulate us into thinking it is still summer but as we fight against the natural rhythm of the season, which is indeed a quiet slow one, we struggle at times to push ourselves when nature is beckoning us to rest and preserve our energy also. As we bustle about, busy in our own little domestic and working worlds, how much attention do we pay to nature at this time? Well for many quite a bit. Feeding the birds on a regular basis, walking in winter landscapes, harvesting our winter vegetables, cutting coppices, clearing rivers and streams of dead weeds from summer, pruning back dead wood from shrubs and trees, mending our fences and walls after autumn gales, and welcoming the Holly King are all activities that show reverence to winter. Nature doesn't waste any energy at this time and we are the only creatures that strain against this, expecting our energy levels to remain pretty constant throughout the year. For some of us winter blues can be a problem. As the amount of sunlight lowers so can the moods of minds not stimulated into action, and such people feel the urge to sleep far longer than the rest of the year. So what connection can we make with the Green Man at this time? Well, evergreens are one such way to keep the relationship going and therefore visiting such trees during winter will help remind us that life does indeed go on in spite of the bleakness around us. The bright red berries of the holly bring cheery spots to forests and woodlands, uplifting the spirit and adding a protective element to our lives if we want it. Traditionally we bring these indoors and deck our halls with them in preparation for the solstice or Christmas celebrations.

This is a time for feasting and giving as we get together with friends and family to celebrate the return of the sun and look forward to longer days to come. The trees may not look or feel any different at this time but their energy is still there just under the surface of the bark, so it is still possible to link up with them throughout winter − but the energy is mellow and less vibrant. My own initiation into trees was a winter one spent walking in the woods with a woodsman who taught me to recognise them by their bark rather than the traditional way of leaf identification. I have since studied the leaves but still rely heavily upon the bark to recognise my friends. It doesn't matter how you get to know trees but access to someone more experienced will definitely make it an easier and more enjoyable experience.

So don't be put off by winter weather. Just wrap up well and make the effort and chances are you will still have some magical moments with the Green Man in winter. Full-moon walks are fantastic all year round but they hold a special magic in winter, especially in the snow, and your chances of spotting wildlife up close are highly probable. Foxes, deer and owls are all very obvious at this time. As we head back toward early spring the energy tide is watery and is a time for cleansing and clearing, so any blockages, problems or illnesses can be helped considerably by meditating on specific trees during this period.

Spring trees

Blackthorn	Birch	Alder
Hawthorn	Hazel	Chestnut
Cherry		

Summer trees

Oak	Willow	Bay
Ash	Hornbeam	Fern
Lime	Sycamore	Palm/date
Maple		

Autumn trees

Elder	Plum	Reed
Apple	Rowan	Damson
Pear		

Winter trees

Holly	Pine	Cedar
Yew	Spruce	

The above lists are simply guides for you to refer to if wanting to know when each tree is at its most energetic, and is open for discussion. The growing season of deciduous trees is by and large the same, with some coming into blossom before others and some bearing fruit whilst others don't etc., but the evergreens are just that, evergreen.

There are many very good tree books about that help to make it easy to identify them that I have recommended in Further Reading.

I argue that we all need to make this spiritual connection with trees for through them we not only understand our environment better and develop a stronger link with nature but we also begin the journey of self-discovery. It is this common human–nature experience that the Green Man wants us to share with him.

FORESTS AND WOODLAND

Like many parts of the temperate world our isles were once very heavily forested areas. Much of this has been cleared for agriculture, housing, roads and industry over the past five thousand years. There are, however, lasting reminders and remnants of these great forests dotted about that we could still visit and make connections with. As a nation we generally hold on to this love of our green spaces and still deep down revere our trees. So let's take a brief look at some of the woodlands, parks and forests you can expect to have a Green Man experience in. To those of you that live in areas I haven't covered I apologise in advance for my choice, as it is restricted to places I know and have visited.

Forests

England's forests are generally found near large estates and either belong or belonged to the Crown or specific landowner. Some of these forests are now managed by trusts or other governing bodies but were once simply land left for deer, boar and other woodland creatures to breed in. This ensured a plentiful supply of game to hunt and in some areas still does.

Epping Forest

Just northeast of London, this massive lung stretches out from Forest Gate in the south to Epping in the north. Once a great hunting forest, this medieval masterpiece is full of history and surprises. During the 1870s the Corporation of London saved Epping Forest from enclosure with the promise that the City itself would foot the bill for its maintenance. Since then it has been managed and conserved by the City of London Corporation as open woodland for the use of the people. Commoners' rights have been upheld and grazing of cattle continued up until quite recently. It was not unusual as a child to find my father photographing cows eating flowers in our front garden before shooing them out. Cattle grids are still evident around the borders of the forest land but unfortunately I haven't seen any cattle loose in the forest since the building of the M11 link road. The dubious practice of hunting foxes with hounds still occurs to the north at Bell Common but elsewhere it has diminished in status as a hunting forest. Many large pollarded oaks, hornbeams and beeches dominate the treescape but there are numerous other species besides. Ponds and lakes such as the Hollow Ponds in the south and Connaught Waters near Chingford allow coarse fishing in season. Queen Elizabeth's hunting lodge can be visited at Chingford but it is the forest itself that really demands our attention. Starting in the south we have the open grassland of the Whipps Cross area interspersed by little wooded spots connecting with Bush Wood. This area is very close to the East End of London and has quite a few roads cutting through it. I wouldn't advise it as a particularly safe place for people to venture through alone but in couples or groups you should be fine. Unfortunately any forested area close to such huge urban development encourages the same highwayman mentality as our ancestors may have encountered in the past. Opportunists are always about so be extra aware of this and be sensible about how you proceed through the forest. This aside, it is still well worth visiting, and if you are interested in characters from the past such as Dick Turpin then a visit to The Wellington public house at Upshire in the northern forest is recommended. The forest scenery changes as we proceed north to High Beech where the trees are now much thicker and just the little roads and sandy tracks make it accessible. This area is quite dense especially as you head towards Theydon Bois and without a map and compass it's likely you'll be lost quite quickly.

I lived in Springfield Farm/Fairmead House at Lippits Hill for a while when young, a wonderful old house and once a lunatic asylum haunted by the ghost of John Clare the poet, a great lover of the forest and nature in general. Most of the treescape is of grassy glades and thicker woodland interspersed by ponds and lakes. There are plenty of human watering holes and tea huts with the headquarters of the conservancy at High Beech behind the Royal Oak pub. This powerful forest captured my heart when very young and to this day, although I've lived and worked in it, I can still get hopelessly lost as it really is quite geographically challenging. One of my favourite places in the forest is Amesbury Banks between Loughton and Epping just off the old A11. This iron age fort was thought to have been used by Boudicca on her way to sack Londinium and a fair few Romans too! The space has amazing energy and the mature beech trees now settled in its heart are great friends of mine. I visit here when I need courage over major issues and have found Boudicca very obliging in a curt and efficient way. Around the Upshire area of the forest you may be lucky enough to catch sight of the illusive shy roe deer that still huddle in quieter spots. Most of the mature trees were once pollarded, a method of cutting lower branches to prevent deer from eating them, but the conservancy policies today seem more oriented towards nature conservation and thinning based on encouraging a wide variety of wild life to live and breed in the woods. Historically Epping Forest is a book in itself, two of which I've recommended in suggested further reading, but as for specific magical spots – well, I'm afraid you will have to find your own by visiting in person one day! Our friend the Green Man is very much alive and well in this place, protecting the space and calling those who love the wild to follow their noses and let him reveal his mysteries to you as you walk. I cannot recommend this place enough but then I should feel this way about my literal roots and hope I always will.

Thetford Forest

Deep in the heart of Breckland lays Thetford Forest, a modern one by all accounts but very much in a style becoming more prevalent in our landscape today. The ancient landscape of bracken moorland and marsh has been drained to allow places such as these to exist. Once the Danish/ Viking capital of East Anglia, Thetford has had a varied history and now most of its population are employed on nearby military bases. The forest itself is predominantly pine and spruce grown for the timber and paper industries but deciduous linear growth is evident along roadsides allowing for a greater variety of wildlife to inhabit the area. Deer roam freely and are seen grazing on the few patches of heathland left dotted about. It covers quite a large area and includes an arboretum amongst its attractions at Lynford. I have several favourite spots in this forest, one being Helen's Well just off the A134 on the way to Grimes Graves, a Neolithic flint mine. This ancient spring sits just below the site of a previous nunnery dedicated to St. Helen or, as it is known more commonly by local pagans, Holda's Well. Another of my frequented sacred places lies at West Stow, where a reconstructed Anglo-Saxon village is accessible and with its lakes and visitor centre it makes for an interesting day out. This area has a very ancient energy to it and is well worth a visit. Warren Lodge just outside Thetford feels very much like the heart of the forest, if you don't mind competing with the noise pollution of modern aircraft flying sporadically overhead. As one of the forests on my doorstep I like to walk in it from time to time and Green Man energy is about if you know where to find it, but I must admit the rows of uniformity can be disheartening for one who prefers a more natural environment. Thetford Forest is accessible from the A134 north of Thetford.

The New Forest

From Southampton in the south to Salisbury Plain, the New Forest is far from new. Like Sherwood it was once one of many royal hunting forests that also came under the protection of the Normans. An ancient system of judicial review stands bi-annually to maintain the conservation of the land and prevent illegal hunting upon it.

Indigenous New Forest ponies breed happily on its heaths and grasslands, so successfully that sadly many are sold off for meat and rarely fetch a good price at auction. Those that are used for riding and driving make excellent pets as they are both hardy and intelligent with a kindly disposition on the whole towards children.

The Verderers and Agisters manage both the needs of the livestock dependent on the forest and the usage by commoners and their ancient rights. The Keepers mainly deal with conservation issues and care for the deer population. Only about half the one hundred and fifty square miles of New Forest is actually wooded and of that some are enclosed for timber production, some anciently preserved and other parts ornamental.

There is great diversity in land and treescape in the New Forest and parts are very magical indeed, especially the more ancient preserved areas of mature oaks and leafy glades. For those of you wishing to visit the forest I'd recommend you allow a few days to fully appreciate its presence and beauty. There are many hotels, B&Bs and camp sites available to suit all needs and pockets. The New Forest can be found at the end of the M3 just southwest of Southampton.

Sherwood Forest

Of all our remaining medieval forests, Sherwood is possibly the most famous and its close relationship with the legend of Robin Hood has made this so. Once part of a much larger royal hunting forest that covered nearly two hundred square miles, it was one of the largest of about ninety such forests in the thirteenth century. Hunting was the preserve of royalty and nobility and was only allowed with permission so poaching became a serious offence that could in extreme or repeated occasions be punishable by death.

It is easy to imagine how resentment grew amongst the lay people of the time. Not only were they prevented from hunting for food but they also had to suffer the huge, often impossible, taxes levied on them. This feudal system was already fixed in place by the time of William the Conqueror, who further yoked the people dependent upon the forest with harsher rules including the prevention of inhabitation and even collection of firewood. Although the legend of Robin Hood fuels our imagination and is disputable in its accuracy one can easily imagine back to the time of these great forests and feel a percentage of young men at least must have braved the consequences of outlaw status if only to affirm their right to freedom. These sons of farmers and foresters would have all the necessary 'tools' for life in the woods and be quite capable of outwitting the local constabulary at every turn if they so wished. It is nice to think they gave their spoils to the poor and maybe such a character as Robin did exist and do just that, but most I presume would have been reduced to criminal status and have ended up as outlaws rather than choosing to be so. The forest is rich with royal history from Henry I to Richard III but by the sixteenth century more land was required for farming and great chunks of the forest were felled. Richer families were also offered portions of it to build their large houses and create their estates on.

One of the biggest tourist draws to the forest today is the legendary Major Oak, believed to be the oldest tree in the park. Although for some time it has been linked with actual usage by Robin and his merry men its longevity doesn't quite stretch that far back and is believed to be about five or six hundred years old. I remember visiting it as a child before the present-day custodians decided to support it and fence it off, and we had great fun playing in and around it. This great old tree still stands as a tangible link and testament to a time long gone.

The forest draws large numbers of visitors to it each year and is well worth seeing and spending some time in. There is definitely a strong Green Man presence in this ancient forest and it has quite a sound underlying energy to it. If you plan a day of quiet walking and meditation I would recommend you avoid weekends, as they can get very busy. Sherwood can be found on the A614 north of Nottingham.

PARKLAND AND ARBORETUMS

Parks are man-made areas of orchestrated beauty combining differing landscapes and trees. These are designed, as opposed to forests that by and large naturally evolved with minimum management. Some of the larger ones were and in some cases still are used for hunting although their main purpose today by and large is for general appreciation. Some of our larger parks are open to the public but some are still privately owned, having some public usage in a restricted way. One name that immediately springs to mind when thinking of English parks is Mr Capability Brown. His landscapes became hugely popular in the eighteenth century and many of our larger estates employed his services to attractively re-design their enormous back yards.

The techniques of drawing the eye to specific locations or towards magnificent lakes or obelisks litter our countryside and can still be observed as you drive around.

Sheep are the main grass cutters in these places and most of them have strong equestrian connections also. In spite of this overtly human intervention the spirit of the Green Man resides in many such places and I must admit doesn't seem too bothered by the deliberate work that goes into maintaining his environment.

Arboretums on first inspection can appear very much like parkland except for one detail, they are collections of specific trees. Each individual has been chosen and sympathetically planted for maximum growth and artistic display. The indigenous breeds grow happily alongside the non-indigenous varieties and are usually representative of either one person's lifetime commitment or a family's love and dedication to acquiring their collections. They are usually at their most stunning during spring and autumn, attracting visitors from far afield by the coachload in some cases, so plan ahead if you want some quiet time in one.

Royal Windsor Great Park

This ancient medieval park belongs to the crown estates but has open public areas for visitors to enjoy. The castle nearby is also well worth going to see whilst you are here, especially if you are interested in our royal history. The history of the park dates back to the time of Edward the Confessor (1042–1066) and was enclosed by the thirteenth century as a hunting parkland for royalty to enjoy. Many ditches or 'pales' were dug at this time as well as fences to aid enclosure. We have already explored the myth of Herne the Hunter thought to have originated from Richard II's time, so I won't linger on it again now, but the spot his oak stood on is marked. The original great park is thought to have once covered over five thousand acres of Surrey and Berkshire but was broken up by the time of King Charles II who also planted the avenue of elms known as The Long Walk. This avenue of mature trees now links the castle with the park itself. In 1580 Lord Burghley ordered the planting of Cranbourne Walk, an act of conservation designed to replenish timber stocks for the navy after the war with Spain. During the seventeenth century one of the park administrators, the Duke of Cumberland, created the Virginia Water, an impressive man-made lake in the southern forest. The great park is landscaped, it must be said, but the forest of Windsor has a wilder feel to it and the spirit of the Green Man is very at home here.

I love the varied landscape of Windsor and can appreciate the grandness of the park with its majestic heritage as much as the solitary aged oaks that are many in this place. It is a great place to explore but allow plenty of time as there is much to take in and one day may not suffice. Cyclists, horse riders and walkers all manage to co-exist, with designated tracks and paths for these activities. Since Victorian times the park has become quite a thriving community with a village and individual cottages for the many and various workers on the estate, so consideration for their living space must be given and respect shown. It is by far the greatest of all our royal forests and holds on proudly to its legacy.

Windsor can be reached by the M4/A335 or by train or bus.

Wanstead Park

This less well-known satellite of Epping Forest was once nothing but a small village served by a lesser manor and remained that way until the turn of the sixteenth century. During this time it was considered large enough to be used as a royal hunting lodge and base for the greater forest. Elizabeth I is said to have been entertained here by the then Earl of Leicester, as were her father and grandfather before her. The park itself bears little resemblance to the grand ornamental landscaping of the late seventeenth and early eighteenth century although some evidence still remains.

Wanstead Park fell into the hands of the Tilney family in 1715, who erected a substantial residence on the site – now just a local golf course. It is still possible to make out the shape of this building from aerial shots and its main avenue of trees leading down to the 'canal' of the ornamental waters which still to this day exists. The house and gardens became showcases of their time but events turned sour and in 1822, due to a poor marriage choice of the then heiress to the estate, one Catherine Tilney, it fell into debt and disrepair. Her husband came with nothing to her bed and took away everything, leaving Catherine no choice but to allow the dismantling and sale of all she owned. She died of a broken heart soon after and is said to haunt the park crying. The disreputable spouse ran off and was not heard of again.

Today the park is managed by the Corporation of London as part of Epping Forest and has for the main part been left to nature. This reclaimed natural oasis is home to many water fowl including herons, grebes and tufted ducks, not to mention swans, and also has a plethora of fauna and flora to see. Bluebell woods, ancient oaks, an old grotto and several ponds can be explored in this most magical of places.

To locate this elusive place you can approach it from Warren Road, London E11, or Wanstead Park Avenue, London E12. I grew up here and this park was my second home: I love it more than simple words can possibly express but an anonymous poem found in William G. Ramsey and Reginald L. Fowkes' *Epping Forest Now and Then* puts it well:

Dear Wanstead Park! What joys are thine,
How many a shady nook,
Where I may at my ease recline,
Or saunter with a book.

The cuckoo shouts his loud clear note
And waits his mate's reply;
The throstle swells her speckled throat,
With songs that pierce the sky.

Across the glade a rabbit runs,
His scut raised high in air,
He thinks he hears the keepers guns,
And hies him to his lair.

Bold robin pipes his cheerful strain,
His notes rise higher and higher,
Alas! He hears a rival's song
His bosom flames with fire.

The blackbird trills a roundelay,
O lovely gush of sound!
Which through the quivering summers day,
Fills the air around.

The linnet flits from tree to tree,
While twittering songs of love,
And hush! There steals across the Lea,
The cooling of the dove.

The insects hum in mazy round,
The leaves are whispering too;
A brown rat glides along the ground,
And disappears from view.

High overhead the solemn crow,
Wheels in his homeward flight,
Then settles on some trees top bough,
As gently falls the night.

Dear Wanstead Park what joys are thine
Through all the changeful year,
Thy beauties to this heart of mine,
Are dear and yet more dear.

Among thy glades the children play,
Light-hearted, happy, free,
Till nature flings her mantle grey,
O'er bird, and flower, and tree.

Long may I know those pleasant glades,
Long may my heart rejoice,
To wander neath the leafy shades,
Entranced by natures voice.

'That voice which never did betray
the heart whose love is true',
So sang sweet Wordsworth in his day,
Dear Wanstead Park – Adieu!

Ickworth Park

This less well known park in Suffolk was once home to the Earl of Bristol, an eccentric man who was heavily inspired by Italian architecture. The house itself with its grand rotunda is pretty unusual even by today's standards but it is the park we will look at. The landscaped gardens were designed by the first Marquess of Bristol in the nineteenth century and are Italian in style. The parkland on the other hand is classic Capability Brown with open glades and carefully placed trees leading to wooded areas, ponds and lakes. Fairy Lake is one such place and is also the source of the River Lark that eventually flows into the Great Ouse north of Cambridge. Presently managed and conserved by the National Trust, the park is open to the public for a small charge and has much to offer seekers of Green Man experiences. There are groves of ancient yew trees and many mature oaks amongst others too numerous to mention. The 1800 acres may take some time to explore and by far the best bits are far over to the left of the house towards Horringer. The park is rarely that busy as most people stick closer to the house rather than venturing farther afield. Deer are kept here in enclosures and sheep, horses and a few cattle also graze its fields.

I strongly recommend you come to Ickworth if you get the chance and get off the beaten track away from the ice cream sellers and play areas to really get a true feel of the place. It is one of my favourite places in this area and has amazing magical energy that is hard to beat. The fairie folk are mischievous here and you do stand a good chance of being pixie-led in this environment, as I know only too well!

You can find Ickworth Park on the A143 just south of Bury St. Edmunds, Suffolk.

Westonbirt Arboretum

This amazing place draws people by the thousand from all over the country, especially in autumn to view its incredible variety of colour and shapes. Captain Robert Holford initiated the Westonbirt collection in the late nineteenth century. Begun as an extension to the existing estate owned by his father, he inherited it ten years after the first planting and continued to pursue his dream with inordinate passion.

One of the most avid collectors of his time he was well placed to achieve his goal due to the huge accessible family wealth he drew upon. He actually commissioned people to hunt out his rare species and bring them back to Westonbirt. The chalky soil gave him a few problems with some trees but even the activities of badgers and rabbits throwing up sandy loam helped him to overcome this and allowed for lime hating species to be grown. One really has to admire the artistic quality of planting and the thought and meticulous planning that went into it. As you enter the park the stunning magnolias and rhododendrons alongside their yew hedge backdrop immediately strike you. The colour combinations are phenomenal but the aromas that permeate the air also bewitch you. The series of rides radiating towards the house were completed in 1875 and entrance all who walk them. Between 1850 and 1875 he also planted his acer glade and Colour Circle that include maples, Katsura trees and Persian ironwoods amongst many others.

I personally love Silkwood as I was privileged enough to ride through it on a daily basis for a few years. The original native oaks and hazel have been carved through to produce these rides with conifers blended in, bringing a refreshing pine aroma to the area.

Since its creation the park has changed hands a couple of times but sadly the family had to relinquish it in 1956 to the Crown in lieu of death duties. Since then it has been managed by the Forestry Commission who do their best to continue the work of the Holfords and have opened it up to public viewing.

As an example of an arboretum Westonbirt is hard to beat and I highly recommend you visit it if you ever get the chance.

The strongest Green Man presence is in Silkwood but the rest of the park is a sensory paradise for all of us to enjoy. It can be found just off the A433 towards Tetbury in Gloucestershire. A true Eden if ever there was one!

WOODLANDS

There are two main types of woodland in this country: preserved woodland and coppiced woodland. These smaller oases of arboreal beauty are dotted liberally all throughout our land. From small copses kept purely for raising non-indigenous pheasants to shoot, to pretty little conserved coppices, we have a plethora of Green Man environments to choose from. Some woodlands are managed, others not; some are cared for by conservation trusts, others left to their own devices, but all have something to offer. Properly run coppiced woodland is sadly in decline as fewer and fewer landowners are prepared to care for them. Luckily some have been rescued by various trusts and are now saved along with the incredible links to our medieval past.

Coppicing is a method of management that cuts the wood growth at stump or, as it is known, 'stool' level about a foot above the ground. By doing this new growth shoots up which in several years' time can be cut again. Coppices are usually managed on area or block rotation allowing for a constant supply of useful wood. Coppice wood, usually chestnut, hazel, ash, alder and willow, can have many uses. Hedging, firewood, besoms, garden furniture, charcoal, fencing and hurdles are all examples of coppice products. Thankfully some people still practise these crafts and in rural areas many of the products are still in demand, making it an almost viable profession, but a hard one! The coppice supports a wide variety of wildlife. Most trust-funded woods are open to the public with organised walks and volunteer days are held regularly.

I discovered the magic of this type of woodland about five years ago and really appreciate the underlying age of these benevolent creatures with their young energy bursting upward each spring. The one I frequent is full of little folk and alive with fairie magic, especially in May when bluebells carpet their way through the hazel, and wild garlic fills the air. Yummy. The Green Man energy is interesting in these places and I

71

find the male energy is quite youthful and fun whilst the Green Lady is older and a great deal wiser. An interesting mix.

I'm not going to cover any individual woodlands as there are literally hundreds to choose from and everyone is likely to be living fairly close to one. There are several web sites listed later on that give you contacts and information about preserved and coppiced woodlands in your area.

'*A Walk*'
Poem by John Clare 1793–1864

The thorn tree just began to bud
And greening stained the sheltering hedge,
And many a vi'let 'side the wood
Peeped blue between the withered sedge;
The sun gleamed warm the bank beside,
'Twas pleasant wandering out a while
Neath nestling bush to lonely hide,
Or bend a musings o'er a stile.

I wandered down the narrow lane
Whose battered paths was hardly dry,
And to the wild heath went again
Upon its wilderness to lie;
There mixed wi' joy that never tires
Far from the busy hum of men,
Among its molehills, furze and briars
Then further strolled and dropped again.

The individual's right to roam has been under attack since the time of the first enclosures, but thankfully many footpaths and bridleways are kept open for our enjoyment. The Ramblers' Association of this country are doing their very best to ensure these ancient tracks are used regularly and not allowed to be blocked by reticent land 'owners'. Local Public Rights of Way officers employed by councils are also working hard on our behalf to achieve much the same result. Whilst it is understandable occasionally that farmers worry about gates being left open and livestock being disturbed it is still our right and is up to each and every one of us to be more proactive in our execution of this 'right' or rite. The majority of walkers are sensible people who just enjoy the countryside in all its seasons and diversity of landscape and are not out to cause any trouble to anyone. Common sense rules the walker who treads sensitively around the edge of a field of crops and it should reflect back on the landowner that helping these people will indeed be beneficial to him or her. I personally have far more respect for landowners who maintain their tracks and stiles than those who turn spare land into a muddy mayhem for motorcycles.

The divide between those who work on the land and those that choose to use it purely for pleasure is a complex one but also one that has mutual benefits to both.

Counties such as Cornwall, for example, rely heavily upon their tourist industry for income these days so it makes sense to help people use the land responsibly rather than creating an 'us and them' situation which could be detrimental to both parties. From my own personal experience Cornwall has the balance just about right. As long as we all show each other respect we can build for the future and as the countryside further evolves new uses and benefits can be found that work well for farmers, tourism and everyday walkers such as myself.

People wanting to embark on an alternative life style and set up temporary camps on roadsides or fields frequently come under attack from many quarters. These so called 'new age travellers' have much in common with all nomadic tribes past and present.

During my life I have encountered several of these 'tribes' and much like all communities they differ widely. Some do show great love and respect for nature and have a great desire to return to a more simplistic lifestyle but are not greeted with joy by the locals they descend upon. Others are less respectful and in some cases quite destructive, causing all travellers to be tarred with the same brush. The 'Donga' tribe and their peace work keep coming up in conversation although I haven't actually met them. It seems that although they may tread on the odd prejudiced toe from time to time but from what I've heard their great work defending nature's right to life is exemplary and your stories travel far and wide. I am sure the spirit of the Green Man/Lady beats true and strong in each and every one of your hearts.'

As we look ahead into the future it seems inevitable that to ensure our survival we must turn away from our current uncontrollable global consumerism and return to a community lifestyle. This can be achieved without the need to take to the road in vehicles or set up camp in benders on muddy fields (not that I have a problem with this, I hasten to add!) but by choosing to buy ethically and when possible locally we are all helping to improve the future. A community that works together and plays together is a happy one, by and large, and although this may be far easier to achieve in villages it is still possible to create mini-communities in towns and cities, indeed it is already happening. The spirit of the Green Man wants us to enjoy his nature for it is our own, and turn away from greed and oppression allowing nature's true balance to return, enriching our lives with harmony, love and understanding.

Lines written in Early Spring
William Wordsworth
1770–1850

> *I heard a thousand blended notes,*
> *While in a grove I sate reclined,*
> *In that sweet mood when pleasant thoughts,*
> *Bring sad thoughts to the mind.*
>
> *To her fair works did Nature link*
> *The human soul that through me ran;*
> *And much it grieved my heart to think*
> *What man has made of man.*
>
> *Through primrose tufts, in that green bower,*
> *The periwinkle trails its wreaths;*
> *And 'tis my faith that every flower*
> *Enjoys the air it breathes.*
>
> *The birds around me hopped and played,*
> *Their thoughts I cannot measure:*
> *But the least motion which they made,*
> *It seemed a thrill of pleasure.*
>
> *The budding twigs spread out their fan,*
> *To catch the breezy air;*
> *And I must think, do all I can*
> *That there was pleasure there.*
>
> *If this belief from heaven be sent,*
> *If such be Nature's holy plan,*
> *Have I not reason to lament*
> *What man has made of man?*

3

Green Man Magic

MAGIC WORKS!

For those of us already consciously practising any form of magic from the illusory to the earth mysteries a realisation occurs. Magic works. Whether you are challenging people's perceptions in an essentially harmless way and simply bringing a little piece of magic into their day or creating spells to gain magical effect, it all counts. There are many kinds of magic and many differing levels. When you mention this word some will tend to think of people like Houdini or more recently David Blaine and the tradition of illusory and endurance magic. This is indeed a valid aspect of the magical world but not all, by a long chalk, as they themselves would probably tell you. Some people will think of mythical magicians and images of Merlin or the ancient Magi spring to mind, and again this is also yet another aspect of magic as it challenges us to believe in the world of myth, legend and adept practices. Then we come to the world of the occult from which yet another branch of magic springs, or several actually, and characters such as Alistair Crowley and Doreen Valiente may enter your head.

In truth the magical world is the world, all of it, as life itself is a form of magic in that it is miraculous and almost defies explanation. So the branch of magic we are continuing to explore is that of nature magic, which in truth is the origin of all subsequent paths.

Trees are gateways to other worlds and also hold great magical power in themselves. Many of our ancestors were aware of this, as are some of us today. So how do you practise the magic of the Green Man?

The most effective way is by direct communication with the environment itself, but there are various forms of language that have developed over time which give you alternative routes. From early shamanic practices discovering the healing properties to our

77

present-day alphabets and the glorious hoard of words that followed, trees were instrumental one way or another in their original discovery.

The world of fairie magic also belongs to this realm and we will peek at these little folk later in this chapter.

There are many branches to follow and some may suit and others less. So it's up to you really. Many of you may be surprised at my inclusion of these languages as they seem confined to divinatory practices today, but I still feel the connection is strong and that it was the energy of the Green Man that inspired them originally.

CELTIC TREE OGHAM

The methods we are going to investigate are some of the most tried and tested communicative paths and we shall start our journey with the Celtic Tree Ogham. For those of you unfamiliar with this I shall explain.

The Celtic Tree Ogham is believed to be the first form of cuneiform writing in the British Isles originating from the Celtic peoples of Ireland and Western Scotland around AD 300–700. Thought originally to be a form of sign language for priests to communicate in secret with one another, it eventually came into more generalised usage.

Its most basic form consists of twenty markings, each representing a particular tree. The markings themselves are straight lines or notches carved either side of an imaginary (or literal) central vertical line. Some are horizontal and others diagonal. These markings formed an alphabet as well as all the many levels of relevance to the tree ascribed. For example, the first on the tree is Birch as represented by a single horizontal right hand mark which lies at the base. So we have the letter B or as written today Beith. This also relates to all aspects of the birch tree. New beginnings, fresh growth, the first, healing, feminine, water etc. to exemplify this further I have included the basic Celtic Ogham in Chapter 6.

I want this present chapter to focus more on magical workings connected with the Green Man.

Three medieval manuscripts have recorded the history of the Ogham and these are the twelfth-century *Book of Leinster*, the fourteenth-century *Book of Ballymote* and fifteenth-century *Book of Lecan*.

The first engravings of these simple markings were found on stones and graves but we can emulate them today by making Ogham sticks.

To do the system true justice I would recommend starting by making a set of your own to use. Ideally you should probably try to obtain a stick from each appropriate tree but failing this you can just pick your favourite and make a set out of it.

Ogham markings are simple and yet take quite a time to become accustomed to as their simplicity becomes oblique when combined, and like any system you are unfamiliar with takes some practice.

Although to replicate them faithfully one should start at the bottom and work up, I have listed them here simply from one through to twenty.

1 ⊢ Birch, B, Beith, water, spring, fertility, beginnings, fresh starts, gentle unfolding, cleansing, purifying, birth, emotional foundations.

2 ⊨ Rowan, L, Luis, Imbolc or early spring, independence, protective, hopeful, generous, increases psychic ability and visionary processes.

3 ⊨ Alder, F, Fearn, fire and water, seen as the spiritual warrior's tree, it offers the shield of the warrior as protection, it is alert yet balanced poised for action, bravery, inner strength and boldness are all qualities associated with alder.

4 ⊨ Willow, S, Saille, water, feminine, unconscious, dream time, emotional flow and emotional healing, the Moon, letting go of negativity, seeing through illusion.

5 ⊨ Ash, N, Nion, all elements, eternal, re-birth, inner child healing, time, a key to the past, present and potential future, the World Tree, when used at Samhain can gain access to ancestors.

6 ⊣ Hawthorn, H, Huath, fire, the may tree associated with romance, love and Beltane, heart chakra, fertility, marriage, sex.

7 ⊣ Oak, D, Duir, fire, the Summer King, confidence, inner strength, courage, physical strength, a door way to other dimensions particularly the world of fairie. Stamina.

8 ⊣ Holly, T, Tinne, fire, the Winter King, survival, protection, gifts and friends, a unifier of souls, cheer and optimism, increases a sense of responsibility.

9 ⊣ Hazel, C, Coll, air and water, the poet's tree, an inspirer, visionary, daydreams, creative, multi-task, intuition, manifests desires, traditionally the dowser's tree.

10 ⊣ Apple, Q, Queirt, abundance, fruitful, generous, healing, selfless, unconditional love, Samhain.

11 ⊹ Vine, M, Muin, summer, group activities, uninhibited, tenacious, connections, teaching, revelry, celebrations, abandonment.

12   Ivy, G, Gort, clingy, attachments, binding, inner searching, choking, restricting, hardy, links.

13   Broom, ng, nGetal, sweeping clean, smudging, astral journeys, 'flying', spring cleaning, living space, aura.

14   Blackthorn, ST/Z, Straiph, protective, obstacles, challenges, banishing, paternal, discipline, order out of chaos.

15   Elder, R, Ruis, feminine, crone, wisdom, experience, soft centred, maternal, giving, versatile.

16   Fir, A, Ailm, long-sighted, rises above problems, horizons, protection, emotionally detached, objective, joyful, peaceful.

17   Gorse, O, Onn, guidance, direction, achievement, rich, sun loving, open and honest, an innovator.

18   Heather, U, Ur, lucky, charitable, passionate, sweet, accepting, tolerant, understanding, loved by bees.

19   Aspen, E, Eadhadh, family, cultural links and communication, speech, song, support, trust, helps face inner fears and grow beyond.

20   Yew, I, Idhadh, death, longevity, ancestral contact, protective, winter, burial on all levels, clairvoyant, mediumship.

There are several ways in which you can make these sticks but my method is to obtain roughly the same length and thickness of stick from each tree first. As a guide to size I would recommend they be about five inches long but you can make them as long or as short as you wish. Then once familiar with each type decide whether to strip them entirely of their bark or leave half of it on.

By using a pen, pyrography iron or heated wire 'mark' each one with its central vertical line. Then follow through by marking each in turn with its appropriate line or lines. Personally I would recommend taking your time over this as it is too easy to just whack out a set without really understanding them. You may wish to make them one a day or one a week or follow through their seasonal connections and really extend the process. You must decide what will work best for you as we all have different learning speeds and only you know how long it will take you. As a general rule as with acquiring all new skills, don't rush it.

So how do you use these sticks once made?

Personally I prefer to roll them wrapped loosely in a cloth and then draw out a specific number and lay them out, but there are other methods and it very much depends just what you plan to do with them. Some people keep them in a bag and draw them much the same way as runes. For simple divination the above method can be employed but for strengthening a magical ritual just one or a specific combination pre-chosen is better. By integrating these magical symbols into our work it is essential that we fully understand them on all levels first and have spent time tuning into their energy in person, by visiting their trees! When planning to use any magical symbol during ritual it is important to give careful consideration as to its desired outcome and application. You can use them to strengthen any magical working merely by placing them on your altar during ritual but to fully incorporate the energy of that Ogham you will need to handle your stick in some way and many people like to pass them through each element before meditating on them. For results magic as in spells, I would stick to using one at a time to start with. Simply by stating something along the lines of

'By the power of Beith I charge thee'

as you send your magical desire into the universe you are adding all the qualities of Birch to your ritual. Don't forget to thank the relevant tree afterwards or better still plant one! This process can be done with any of the Ogham if you so wish but please take it seriously as negative repercussions can also result if one hasn't examined any potential spell properly in advance. You don't have to be specifically following the Celtic tradition to use the Ogham but it would obviously help.

The best way to familiarise yourself with each of the Ogham is by a process of gradual meditative assimilation. This will ensure that any lessons are learnt and that your subconscious has a firm grasp of the symbol/s you plan to work with.

The Tree Ogham may well have been where the expression 'pulling the short stick' came from and in some respects makes sense. You could all agree beforehand which Ogham is 'the short stick' and go from there in the normal fashion. It's a thought.

The Tree Ogham and all its deeper spiritual and directly arboreal connections had been well established for a great time. The runes of the Norse also have their tree relationships. Although these were part of a greater belief system they were still very closely linked to trees.

THE RUNES

Modern runes owe their origins to our Scandinavian and Anglo-Saxon cousins who first brought them to our shores. Like the Ogham, runes were once a form of alphabet and many standing stones in places such as Jutland in Denmark carry such markings.

The word 'rune' is thought to have meant many things, from basic communication to inner secrets and/or discussions. It is impossible to define exactly where and when the first runic markings were designed and/or used but suffice it to say they are western European in origin and were probably in use by the first millennium BCE. The Odinic myth of the northern tradition claims that Odin hung himself upside down from an ash tree for nine days and nights, during which time the mystery of the runes was revealed to him. There are many different runic systems but the one we shall look at is the most easily learnt and commonly used and that is the Elder Futhark. This consists of three parts or Aetts (meaning a group of eight) and is divided into twenty-four (sometimes twenty-five) runes. Runes were probably first created by scratching marks on stones or split branches but the majority of sets made today are created from cut wooden or clay tablets. Each rune has its own tree association and indeed many people link them with specific flowers and gemstones although this is a modern practice.

First Aett

F	ᚠ	Feoh	Cattle, wealth (or as in today liquid assets)
U	ᚢ	Ur	Ox (Aurochs), primitive physical strength, well being
Th	ᚦ	Thorn	Thorn, protection, phallus
A	ᚨ	As	God/male energy, divinity
R	ᚱ	Rad	To ride, motion, travel
K	ᚲ	Ken	Torch or guiding light, to see (as in understand)
G	ᚷ	Gyfu	Gift, love, exchange
W	ᚹ	Wyn	Happiness, joy, uplifting

Second Aett

H	ᚺ	Hagal	Hail, delays, interruption, making form
N	ᚾ	Nyd	Need/s, basic, requirements
I	ᛁ	Is	Ice, preserve, static
J	ᛜ	Jera	Harvest, summer, seasons, judgement
E	ᛇ	Eoh	Defence, bows, yew, protection
P	ᛈ	Peorth	Fate, initiation, re-birth, womb
X	ᛉ	Elhaz	Elk, power, direction, resolute
S	ᛋ	Sigel	Sun, light, victory, unified

Third Aettt

T	ᛏ	Tyr	God Tyr, arrow or sword, warning, sacrifice
B	ᛒ	Beorc	Birch, beginnings, cleansing, healing

E	ᛗ	Ehwaz	Horse, transport, cooperation
M	ᛗ	Man	Humanity, identity, self
L	ᚱ	Lagu	Goddess/water, emotions, flow
Ng	ᛉ	Ing	Divine force/orgasm
O	ᛩ	Odel	Family, ancestors, home
D	ᛟ	Dag	Daylight, dawn, noon, rotation.

So now you have either made or bought your first set of runes what do you do with them? Well it's up to you really, as their uses are many. Some people like to use them for divination by placing them in a bag and drawing them out individually, as in a specific number, and placing them deliberately, but the preferred method is to grab a random handful and just throw them down. The upright ones relate to those things that are obvious or open and the others to that which is hidden or not immediately obvious.

The ones nearest to the person are things happening now or the past and the ones farther away are likely to manifest unless changes are made now. I have a friend who has made a nice elemental cloth to cast her runes on. The cloth has a black background with a large circle on it divided into four. Each sector represents earth, air, fire and water and is colour coded. She places the cloth aligned to north when using it and takes the combination, or lack, of the rune and element into account when reading, i.e. if you were to throw an upright Is rune on to the water element one could surmise that ice will form and that this person is feeling cold and detached or that there is too much emotion for them to handle. It really is quite simple once you become familiar with the symbols and if you are brave you can expand your set by adding further Anglo-Saxon runes. A couple of good books are recommended in further reading if you wish to follow this path further.

What else can a layman use runes for?

Look around you where you live and chances are you will find runes. They have been traditionally incorporated into architecture by the use of differing shades of brick for centuries. Near where I live there is a Regimental Museum and it has spectacular Ing runes on its tower. Early Anglo-Saxons would either carve or mark their houses with protective runic markings for a variety of reasons. We all need protection and whether it be from a known enemy or ill health it's better to be safe than sorry. Many people like to make a runic pendant or lucky charm to wear and these can be most effective.

But how can a simple marking on a piece of wood hold any power or magical energy? Through their repetitive usage and the belief by the user that they do. Runes have been used for longer than our present-day alphabet and I don't think any of us would argue that words in themselves can carry great power. A lot depends on the intent, the desire and the belief.

It is also possible to use runes as a form of language and therefore, should you wish to, you can literally write with runes, for example.

So what about their tree connections?

The first Aett

Going back to the first Aett we have Feoh, the rune of wealth or material possession. This rune is thought to be associated with elder, a tree we tend to think of as a prolific invader at times. This magical tree gives its flowers (used for elderflower wine or juice) and berries for the same each year. The wood has a hollow pulpy centre easy to work and therefore can be used for making pipes and/or beads amongst other things. the elder is a tree of wisdom gained over time and therefore links with crone or elder energy. It is thought to be unlucky to bring it into the house but I haven't found any real substantiation of this superstition. One presumes the Feoh rune and elder work together, as we all should become wiser over time where money is concerned. To ask the elder for help meditatively over material issues can be beneficial.

The rune Ur has birch as its tree, which may surprise you, as one would not necessarily associate them together; but if we consider that birch is first to take hold on new ground then that is its strength. The birch tree has quite durable wood once dried and can be used for many purposes including the making of besoms. Its physical properties are many, as are its healing abilities, so this watery tree can spring up anywhere and survive. Drinking birch tea made from leaves is a great anti-toxicant, especially for kidneys. Birch is the tree of ultimate cleansing and well-being. It also connects with first love of the feminine or mother love.

The three trees I have found associated with thorn are hawthorn, bramble and blackthorn, for fairly obvious reasons. The thorn rune represents the sharp prick or scratch of these thorny trees and yet they also hold other powers. Hawthorn is connected to the sexual aspect of thorn and is useful in love magic. Bramble also shares this quality with an added fruitfulness or fertility. Blackthorn is a protector and a darker aspect of thorn, as blackthorn will cause quite a stir if provoked. Anyone who has been unlucky enough to receive such a scratch or similar knows what I mean! I haven't as yet, but I do treat this tree with utmost respect.

Ash and lime are the trees I've found connected with the rune As. Ash contains all elements and therefore makes it well placed to be a divine or direct channel for the As rune. Lime trees or linden trees were once specially grown to resemble the World Tree more associated with the ash. This combination is an eternal one of birth, life and death so linking its godlike status, but lime is traditionally linked with Freyja so it seems the dualistic approach of using both for magical workings would prove more potent and definitely suitable for those of Wiccan persuasion.

Rad is one of many runes linked with the oak tree. As a spiritual messenger oak opens doorways to other worlds and one can argue Rad is the energy necessary to travel into these worlds. Rad allows movement and yet one has to be best placed at the time to make the most of its energy. Oaks are great directors and sitting with one will help focus your intent and channel your energy deliberately. Rad and oak used together will maximise any project, desire or plan as long as you put the required effort in.

Next we meet up with Ken, linked with the pine tree. These trees are thought to be great for showing the way or lighting up the path ahead. Using incense made of pine bark or resin will aid understanding and much will be revealed to you by this illuminator. Pine trees are one of the oldest species on the planet and as such have seen all. This places them in the best position to aid understanding and clear the head. Pine is traditionally used for air freshening as it works subtly to clear unpleasant smells and also has the effect of helping us to think more clearly.

And now for Gyfu: its tree is ash. The two symbols that construct this rune combine the dualistic meeting of two worlds that of Middle Earth and Asgard. By opening to the heart of Gyfu we open to ourselves and link divinely. Ash is the World Tree and connects on all levels, so is a door for the gift of love to flow through. Split ash trees are great for healing and initiation workings.

The last rune of this Aett is Wyn and its tree is also ash, for to really appreciate the loving Gyfu we need to be prepared to expand. Wyn is this love expressed in its fullest form of complete happiness and contentment. The ash tree is such expansion, for although it takes its time to leaf in spring it nurtures loving energy slowly, being prepared to take its time and wait. As above and so below is the message of ash. All should be harmonising naturally for happiness of Wyn to shine through.

The second Aett

The first rune is Hagal and its tree is the yew. This rune is female and contains transformative power to both destroy and heal. It works well with the yew as an evergreen that internalises life and death eternally. For like the hail that Hagal can bring the yew can also poison. Awareness of both the power of the yew and Hagal can help us take stock of our present space and actions. Winter is both preserving and yet unpleasant at times, as can be the effects of Hagal, but we need these natural functions to slow us down at times.

Nyd is associated with both the rowan tree and the beech tree. Rowans are great survivors and often solo encouraging us to meet our own Nyd or needs. Be yourself is the message here, be true to your own wyrd. The benevolent beech is a communicator of this Nyd and enables us to express ourselves tolerantly without prejudice. The Nyd or basic requirements for life are often over-complicated and therefore both the rowan and the beech can help clear the dead wood and realise that which is most important over that which is most definitely superfluous.

The tree associated with the next rune Is is alder. This almost waterproof wood grows near rivers and streams and appreciates the need of this element whilst protecting itself from becoming soft like a birch. It is a tough uncompromising tree that recognises the Nyd or necessity without waste and like ice can preserve for long periods if required. Alder wood is tough and hard compared with many of our native species, as is the effect of this rune at times. Often known as the spiritual warrior's tree, it says focus on the now, look at what you've got and protect it.

Jera is a rune of harvest and is linked with oak. It represents the cosmic order utilised to gain effect. It only has effect if the person goes with the natural flow of the seasons and like the oak will slowly gain strength. Its energy is dynamic but cyclical and therefore relates to the old adage 'what goes around, comes around'. The oak tree in conjunction with Jera will add longevity and structure to one's plans whilst helping you to achieve your goals in a fairly structured manner.

Eoh is another rune linked with the yew tree. It is a harbourer of death and was often most commonly used for the making of bows. The harvest of Jera once reaped is often seen in a sacrificial way and there-fore both the yew and Jera represent this eventual inevitability. It asks us to face death and also accept it as a part of our shared life experience. Many shamanic techniques use yew and through such practices can access the underworld and world of fairie and seemingly survive. It connects with Christ and Odin.

Aspen and beech are trees most often linked with Peorth, the womb of life. Aspens are amazing trees, often with connecting roots that create one that are in fact many. Beech is feminine and links with gestation or the potential hidden from view. Both these trees have the ability to link up with the subconscious and act as vessels for initiation but the dice of life often throws up unexpected events we haven't bargained on, so using Peorth with either beech or aspen will help you move through a difficult patch. Peorth is power made manifest.

Elhaz is yet another rune connected to the yew tree and as such is one of the most powerful protective symbols. It relates to the elk and is defensive, much like the yew, and can ward off unwanted attention. To use this symbol as a protection is most effective, especially if carved on to yew wood. The protection will work eternally or as long as you choose to use it, much as the yew tree itself.

The last rune of this Aett is Sigel and its tree is the bay tree. This powerful male rune links with solar energy and like the bay thrives in warm sunny conditions. Bay is a wonderfully aromatic tree and has great culinary uses but magically its use is one of increasing male force. It represents triumph of light over dark and as such the bay tree can also thrive in these intensely light situations. Sigel also relates to lightning or a sudden blast of light and the peppery taste of bay certainly is hot if allowed to fully flourish.

The third Aett

Tyr's tree is the oak again and like its tree it demands space to act in. The god Tyr sacrificed his hand in order to save cosmic order from the destructive force of the Fenris wolf and as such oaks will sacrifice limbs if needed in order to maximise their life span. The oak accepts this as necessary and so does Tyr. We all have to do what we have to do to get to where we want to be but not without a little self-sacrifice along the way.

The birch tree is next and corresponds with Beorc. This feminine tree represents new beginnings and birth, as does Beorc. It is very helpful in use with healing women's problems and can aid health, especially in delivery. The two points are breasts from which the milk of life flows and birch too flows with life-enhancing sap which we can drain off and drink. Birch leaf tea will aid de-tox and general inner cleansing. It is great when used to mark a new start especially for women.

Both ash and oak link with Ehwaz, the rune of the horse. Today we can link up these trees and this rune with all modes of transport over land but horses are still its main power source. To ride a horse requires cooperation between horse and rider. This corresponds with our need for safe transport versus the risk we take when venturing forth in such a manner. Trust and loyalty are encouraged by the bravery of oak and the cosmic order of ash. We must be genuine in intent and sure of destination when using this rune and its tree connections.

Man, the rune of humanity, is connected with maple, alder and holly. These trees, although quite different, all represent cycles of our shared human experiences. Maple responds to our emotions and desires, alder to our collective needs and strengths and holly to our eternity or future legacies. By combining these runes into a bind rune one can utilise their power for global magic but I personally think this sort of working is potentially dangerous unless one treads very carefully. Using them to ask for world peace or greater tolerance is probably safe, however.

The Lagu rune is essentially feminine and is combined with the willow tree and the moon. This tree and rune are perfect bed partners as willow prefers a watery home and Lagu is water. All female mysteries and energies can be worked by using the Lagu rune in conjunction with willow. Its roots are resilient and fast growing, the trunk can sprout forth with new growth even when fallen and the leaves are most efficient at making the most of any given situation. Much like women really.

Ing, the rune of pure divine force, has the apple tree as its arboreal friend. I find this interesting for whilst Ing represents the safety and comfort of home it also relates to the orgasm – and what do we normally associate with apples? The apple tree is a beneficent tree of life giving fruit but biblically it was linked with knowledge. The northern tradition also thinks of Ing as being a portal to greater understanding and divine messages. Arguably Ing or its force came from the east and travelled west, indicating a new introduction of skills and ideas entering our country from Europe at some point. Apples are also linked strongly with love and our indigenous fruits were crab apples. As we bred them selectively the taste became more palatable so it seems to eat of the fruit gave us access to our own divine sexual power through Ing.

Odel, the rune of the family and ancestors, links with the loving and protective hawthorn. This tree is still used as hedging and is a most effective barrier whilst having many generous healing attributes. Without the power of hawthorn calling us to love and give to one another we wouldn't be here at all so the link is basic and functional. The thorns of hawthorn protect the love from attack whilst its flowers ensure fertility and its fruit although bitter is honest in representing birth and child rearing which can be a bitter sweet pill for all.

The last rune of this Aett and the Elder Futhark is Dag and is linked with oak and spruce. The rune of daylight or the return of the sun is an uplifting rune and contact with both spruce and oak is also most elevating at times. Oak spreads to receive light whilst spruce reaches ever upwards. They call us to embrace the light as our source of energy and be re-vitalised by it.

And so ends our little excursion into runes and their arboreal links with the spirit of the Green Man. I totally believe that our ancestors' daily relationship with trees was far stronger and more spiritually intimate than ours today but for many of us the love, energy and knowledge is being sought out. It is very easy to blindly follow these old ways but we really need to make our own individual connections with trees to fully understand and appreciate a little of what they can offer us today.

Last night was a mid-month harvest moon and I ventured forth to a local park. Although much magic occurred my most memorable experi-ence was standing amongst several large mature yew trees. The protective warmth these trees offered was much appreciated, especially after an hour of screeching owls and panting wolves. One immediately understood why we feel safe in their environment but you have to do it yourself to really feel it.

OFFERINGS AND RESULTS

By far the most common form of magical act any of us can indulge in is the giving and receiving aspect of what is now recognised as results magic. Some people may like to think of this as spell casting and in some respects they are right, but as with anything we wish for in life we must be absolutely sure we really want the intended effect to manifest, because it will! There is a very old and wise saying that totally applies to this type of practice and that is 'Be careful what you wish for – it might just come true'. And so it is with trepidation and caution we tread this path. Even the simple act of leaving an appropriate offering to a tree can have enormous results if you really desired 'something' whilst making this symbolic sacrifice. It is not always easy to foresee events and understand every single implication of your actions until it is too late so I advise you as follows.

1. Deeply consider the intended result and whether you really want it.
2. Take full responsibility for *your* actions.
3. Try waiting at least one moon cycle before committing to it; you might find reason/s not to go ahead after all.
4. Accept the result as being what nature has responded to.

Armed with this knowledge you can now explore nature magic in all its elements. So what can you do? Well the most simple and effective method is as follows.

1. Decide what you wish to achieve; for example, 'I want more confidence'.
2. Choose where you wish to magically ask for it; for example, you could visit your favourite oak tree.
3. Decide when you want to carry it out. For instance, what time of day, day of week or moon cycle. As a general guide the new moon to full moon period will draw that which you wish to you; a waning moon will rid you of things or cleanse; a dark moon is good for divination or seeking new light on your path.
4. Visit this place either with some sort of offering (non-toxic) or decide in advance what you are prepared to do in return, such as offer a gift or gratuity to a conservation group, do voluntary work or plant a tree.
5. Just sit down in peace with your space and chosen tree and ask inwardly or outwardly for that which you desire, affirming your request and thanking the tree afterwards.

It really can be that easy but you must above all else *believe*!

If you already practise any form of meditation or spiritual energy raising techniques then the effects may well be deeper and more profound. Spending quiet time 'feeling' or, as some put it, 'tuning in' to the energy of the space also intensifies the desired result. The old cliché of 'People can only love you, if first you love yourself' applies equally to the spirit of the wild wood and having a certain level of self esteem and worth does help considerably. Belief in one's abilities also helps the movement of magical energy; in fact one could say it is paramount to success. Being prepared and willing to befriend your environment and the trees within it unconditionally in an accepting but open way strengthens the bond between you and adds to the effect.

Understanding the elements, cycles of nature and seasonal energy variations helps consolidate that which you wish to achieve.

If you can master these levels of awareness then your results will be more effective but you might also find this type of magic completely unnecessary, as your very presence may be enough to make the magic happen.

To exemplify this further let me explain. One of my magical friends and I often venture out on moonlit nights to the woods at the back of his house. Each time we go more 'magic' happens. From visual images such as twenty-foot high dragons to lions appearing in trees, you name it, we've probably witnessed it and can well understand how it must have put fear into many minds in ancient times. These apparent manifestations are by and large created by the effect of the moon's light, but as you accept them and stay focused upon them they usually define into three-dimensional form, again something that doesn't rest easy with everyone, but we love it and try to take note of all that we see. Yes I know what you are thinking, 'they are hallucinating' and maybe we are; but jointly? The magic doesn't stop there: we've experienced audible magic too, such as the panting of wolves and smells that are quite out of place, so each sense is being tested under these conditions and all perceptions widened as a result.

We always ask the spirit of the Green Man for permission to enter beforehand and if we get a negative response we have learnt from experience it is best to adhere to this.

FAIRIE MAGIC

Yes I believe in fairie folk and that may have some of you chuckling or questioning my sanity, but for me these energies are very real. It's true as a child they were nothing more than entertaining stories and the 'real' connection has been made since but, now that it has, I believe. I wanted desperately to experience their energies when little but was so full of fear and doubts it's not surprising that it didn't happen for me. What I didn't realise then, but do now, is that you have to totally believe in order for them to exist for you in the first place. So what exactly am I talking about? Are we about to enter the world of little flying people and pixies with pointy ears? Yes literally if you want to.

Are these really physical manifestations of an overactive imagination? No, not quite. The world of fairie has lived in the hearts of our woodlands, rivers and wild places as much as it has in our own true hearts since well before recorded history. I don't believe for one second somebody just made them up one day and that was that. There are too many similarities between our fairie folk and the little people of other countries for that to be true. I also don't believe for one second that they are extra-terrestrial beings of grey skin and big black eyes that fly saucers about the universe.

What I do believe is that they operate in a gateway world between ours and another dimension. This may well sound outlandish to those of you that come from a purely scientific viewpoint or see such suggestions as pure fantasy and insubstantial, but the world of fairie can be accessed if you really want to glimpse it.

The fairies of my favourite places vary considerably from little lacewing slithers of magical light to naughty pixies whose voices can be heard laughing at you but are very rarely seen. There are the black elves who live in caves and usually come out at night and light elves who sprinkle their fairie dust leading your eyes to where they want you to focus when out walking in day time.

So what exactly is fairie magic?

This is very difficult to explain as one has to believe in them in order for it to happen for you anyway. As tiny personifications we link them with children and it is true that the link is often made when very young. As an experiment try asking how many under-fives have had fairie encounters and I think the percentage will be quite high. But many adults still believe and keep the connection going as can be seen by the inordinate number of fairie stories still written and of those that have gone before them. Deep down in all of us fairies challenge our inner child's perspective and if we do let ourselves totally believe, even for a brief time, the seed can be sown for future experiences.

Fairie magic is unique and very powerful and as such should be entered into with a great deal of respect for this magical realm of creative opportunities. Here in the west it is becoming increasingly difficult for people to express their creative outlets as many schools and education departments have reduced all forms of art to non-core status. Therefore, it seems, only children encouraged by their parents can still expect to flourish and bring out their best. When my daughter was old enough to start school we sent her to a private school, much to the horror of my own family and many of my more left-wing friends. This wasn't an act of overt snobbery on our behalf. It was because on investigating and touring all the schools and options in our area this one held the principles I felt were most important to my child's development. The then headmaster, a jolly enthusiastic chap, proved to me beyond all doubt that he wasn't hugely worried about competing in local results and tables of academic achievements. What he really strived for was to bring out the best in each child, to recognise the spirit within and encourage it to follow its own path, and if that meant he had a mixed bunch then so be it. My daughter loved her time spent at the school and had the best formative start any child could possibly have and yes, she is very loving, compassionate, imaginative and creative. As I mentioned earlier we are inadvertently or otherwise suppressing creativity and imagination in today's western culture but by connecting with fairie magic you can begin to bring it back.

This magic is as old as time itself, maybe even older, and the energies you may encounter have very little to do with people. These are elemental forces and therefore pretty primitive. They aren't in the least bit interested in our everyday nonsense because to them that's what it is, nonsensical. In the realm they come from all things are possible as this is a very imaginative dimension. From this realm our origins lay much like the dormant energies of trees in winter just waiting to be sprung loose again.

So how can you make a start?

Well first, if you have a garden, you can try encouraging them into your space by making it attractive to them and thinking of them when looking after it. They prefer quiet undisturbed places best and traditionally like wildflowers rather than modern hybrids. Toadstools are fun and appreciated so try putting some around; whether ceramic or wood, they like them and will often surprise you by manifesting the real thing at a later date. This is a sign of acceptance and their way of saying, 'hello'. They love wild roses, honeysuckle, primroses, bluebells, ivy, birch, willow, oak and elm amongst many others besides. They don't like enforced management of the space, rubbish or waste, and anything vaguely toxic or harmful to nature will put them off. Having a water bath for the birds also encourages them, as does feeding birds in winter. Butterflies are often drawn to fairie places in great numbers, probably due to the flowers, but sometimes it can seem magical to watch great numbers of them swirling about almost like the very fairies themselves.

Sitting in your fairie spot hoping to 'see' them is probably at best a futile exercise but sitting near the spot with love and wonder in your heart will start the magic going. If you do catch a glimpse of them they frequently disappear instantly and very few people get to view them openly, as they are a little shy and very cautious. My fairie spot in the garden has strengthened over the past few years since I moved to my current home and is fast becoming a portal to their realm. How can this be, you may ask, or how do you know this? It comes to us when we least expect it and many times this spring and summer whilst sitting at my table either reading or writing I find myself drifting to another world of magic and mystery. This place varies considerably and often links to real places as if invisible threads of pure loving energy are pulsating between these three dimensions. This could be construed as basic daydreaming but it's not as such and has a different feel about it. I rarely retrace any definable thought processes to seek the origin of these visions or happenings but when I do there is usually one key that triggers it into action and that is the key of love. Simply by opening your heart to nature's wonders and beauty, this magical effect can begin to manifest. This may still seem bizarre or unreal to you so let me give an example.

One day I sat in this spot and an image of a river came to me with willow trees and a lush grassy bank. I saw a man casting something from his hands into this river. He had such sadness in his eyes. I felt a profound connection with his feelings as they were of sacrifice and he was obviously making some sort of offering to the spirit of the river.

It was as though the spirits of the fairie folk around me linked with this spirit and wanted me to share this moment. After this experience I felt a little confused but a week later I met up with the man himself and discovered that he'd indeed done such a thing and he seemed quite surprised I'd picked up on it, especially as at the time I witnessed it he'd only thought of doing it. So in other words they let me witness an act about to happen rather than glimpsing into the past literally. Some of you may say this was perhaps a form of psychic connection between me and this man, which indeed may well be true, but I also felt strongly that it was the world of fairie that allowed this vision to manifest rather than a direct personal link.

This is only one limited example as fairie magic has far more to offer than linking us with other people. The most potent form of fairie magic I've experienced is that of divine art or creation itself. Many people connected to the world of fairie are young at heart it must be said but they are often the most originally inspired folk. The woods I link up with on this level are amazingly beautiful and lovingly managed in a traditional and sympathetic way. The magic is active all year round, in spring the fairies themselves are very prevalent amidst the wild garlic and carpets of bluebells and it is at this time that I find myself most inspired to write and paint. In summer the lushness of the new greenery is full of magical scents and butterflies, and pixies have fun challenging our perceptions in a deliberate ruse to lose you in their kingdom. Two years ago I sat under a fairie tree quietly for some time and as I went to leave I became aware of a coiled grass snake sunning itself less than three feet from me. I had no idea how long it had been there and it didn't seem bothered by my presence at all. This was fairie magic and a moment I will always feel privileged to have witnessed. By autumn the elves are busy spreading the seeds and the air is thick with potential fertility for the next season, whilst we wonder at the changing leaves and are blown about with them. This season inspires communication on all levels and for me is often the time I feel I want to be creative in a more earthy way either by crafting wands and staffs or attempting to construct besoms. Last season I made two prototypes, my first effort at this ancient art, and spent a blissful day on my own in the woods with a fire going making my brooms. To me they were just brooms, normal average besoms, but I'd been pixied or elved – I'm not too sure which – and my perceptions had been well and truly challenged. They were eight-foot tall monsters, fit for giants, something I really didn't notice until it was time to go home and put them in my little car. Ooops. This caused huge amusement to many, though, and I did manage to trim them down to near normal size after, but it's an example of how easily we can lay ourselves open to magic and how funny it can sometimes be! They must have gleaned much amusement watching me bimble about all day oblivious of what I was really achieving.

In winter the black elves pop up and protect the woods, giving very clear messages as to where they are happy for you to tread and where not. The creative flow slows down but I quite like this as more consideration is given to most of what I do at this time. My work may take a little longer but the results can often be that much better for it.

This winter I will be turning my attention to poetry once this work is finished, inspired by the winter landscapes to come.

Your own fairie connections may well be quite different from mine but will be pertinent to you on a deep level and more often than not it manifests as love expressed. This isn't necessarily the human love for another, but a love of creation itself, and by experiencing their energies you can open up new or dormant parts of yourself to creativity.

One only has to look at the inordinate amount of poetry, prose, art and song that fairie folk have inspired to realise this is a world of infinite possibilities. So on a very basic level how can one make a start?

- First you need a fairie spot or place to focus on or just be in.
- Think like a child, be full of wonder and fully appreciate the beauty of all you see.
- Feel love, inwardly and outwardly.
- Have only pure intentions.
- Keep your own impact on the environment to its minimum.
- Be respectful.
- Don't stare.
- Take an offering.
- Believe.

Do all these things enough and a connection with the world of fairie will be made, not always obviously at first, although you could be lucky, but often subliminally.

Before we leave the fairies a quick word about gnomes. Contrary to popular belief gnomes are not fairie folk as such. *Genomus* means earth dweller or, more simply put, the earth elemental; but offering it money, semi-precious stones or such like will aid you in prosperity.

There are specific days and times that are considered auspicious for fairie magic and these are fire festivals, May eve, midsummer's night, dawn, noon, twilight and midnight, and full moon.

WARNING

There are many people who still choose to believe it is possible for us to be literally kidnapped or taken away by fairies and many old wives' tales will insist this is so. Tales of people entering their world to help as midwives or be given magical gifts abound throughout history and it is not for me to dispute this possibility. I go on my own experiences and personal perceptions but felt it was valid to include this warning as a safeguard. Roses or rose oil is believed to protect you from abduction by little folk.

As for being pixie-led, yes I have been once or twice!

THE MAGICAL HEART

All of us have a heart, that organ under our ribs that beats rhythmically, pumping our blood or life force around our bodies. Trees may not have an actual individual organ that carries out the same function but they do have sap rising and falling throughout their lives carrying the vital nutrients for their being. And so by comparison we reflect upon the concept of a magical heart and wonder at its incredible nature. Pure spirit exists as the spark to start the heart on its journey and soon grows, strengthening as it does. Sometimes it has to pump harder, other times less so, occasionally it is challenged by outside influences that may contaminate or threaten it but still it beats.

The magical heart of the Green Man can be found in many places from the humble houseplant to the wild rainforests and every green place in between. So whether you want to work indoor magic or get outside into his more challenging environment you will still be able to feel his rhythm. Science now knows that we influence everything we look at or focus upon and that merely by observation we alter the movement of the smallest particles. This isn't to say we are special or elevated to a higher plane because of this new awareness, just that we can conceptualise it intellectually. The power of cognitive thought seems reserved for humanity, but is it? In truth we don't really know and as far as the magical heart is concerned it doesn't really matter, as it will still beat on regardless. I once watched a documentary on our solar system and the scientists who had produced it played to us the rhythm of our own sun. This amazing sound still reverberates deep inside and moved me to tears when I heard it as it was our own beat, steady, pulsating unrelenting and most of all it felt safe. Our earliest memories are of our mother's heartbeat and resonate deeply within all of us as a time when we felt secure and most loved. As we grow up we come to terms with our own inner rhythm and how it responds to those around us, but the closest we can get to the nature of our magical heart is by opening ours to each other and to nature.

For me the more remote or wild a place is, the stronger this heart beats in its purest form, almost untouched by our hands in wild woods, mountains and jungles far away. This is the spirit of divine creation, pure and untainted as nature intended. The magical heart of such wild places will definitely have the most profound effect on your human psyche but you can also experience it closer to home. It seems apparent to me that our relationship with this heart can vary considerably. In wild untouched places it sounds loudest and fills us with magical love. In our fields and woodlands it harmonises with our own heart and we feel a contact of mutual love. But in dark forgotten industrial wastelands it struggles much like we do just before our own death and can only beat faintly and is almost imperceptible at times.

So what is the magic of the heart and how do we work it?

To do this we need to strip away everything and journey inwards towards our essence. There are many ways in which one can do this, from hermitic isolation to purging or gradual meditations and/or path workings. Questions you might want to pose to yourself are 'who am I?' or 'what makes me tick?' and 'when do I feel most alive?' these sorts of profound inner mysteries are simply tools for getting you started on your journey but everyone has to start somewhere.

Just by linking ourselves to certain trees and finding our spiritually arboreal heart we can learn more about ourselves than any psychologist is likely to.

Are you someone who likes a fast pace of life? If so you could resonate with the faster growers such as pine, spruce, eucalyptus and leylandi.

Do you prefer a steady pace? If so you might be drawn to lime, hazel, ash or alder trees.

If you embrace a slower pace then oak, beech, yew or sequoia may beat to your rhythm.

These links between the speeds of growth are significant, as they will reflect your own desires and inner harmonies at this time.

The very best way of all though to discover your inner Green Man and your magical heart is by deciding what type of environment draws you to it the most.

Choose a day, or night, to visit such a place and just wander. If possible try not to be restricted by time limits and if a week of camping is required then organise it and go for it. The best way in which to approach this is to just bimble about aimlessly, following your own heart. Let the space direct you; if a tree draws you to it during your walk then sit with it and just be. Don't expect anything or assume much and soon a loving beat will flow between you. You may be drawn to many trees of differing types but take note of any that have a profound feeling of love, safety and security, for this or these are your magical heart. Try and leave the outside world behind and just for the moments you share forget all your worries and external concerns. All that matters is your heart opening to the heart of the new friend you have found. Don't worry if it isn't a tree that draws you: nature's spirit may resound stronger through the animals, plants and birds of your space than any particular individual tree. But unless you have chosen the sea, a desert or frozen environment then there are bound to be some trees nearby that you can see.

This ancient way of finding your magical tree can in some ways be likened to the totemic system in its method but can also be quite happily integrated.

Once you have discovered which type of tree you feel most at home with you can take it a step further to strengthen the relationship. There are so many ways in which you can express this new love and it would be silly to dwell on it as most should be obvious to you. The most fulfilling experience will be frequent bonding sessions but all levels can be explored.

1. What was it that drew you? For example, beauty, energy, colour, smell.
2. What type of tree? For example, deciduous, evergreen, small, large.
3. What did you feel with it? For example, love, peace, relaxed, inspired.
4. What do you feel you have in common with it? For example, strength, individuality, expressiveness, resilience.

5. How have you been since? For example, uplifted, happy, exhilarated, healed.

These are a few questions you might like to ask of yourself after first encountering your tree and connecting with your magical heart. This type of tree will mean something to you and it might take time for you to realise this, but reading up on all of the tree's qualities on every level will give you more to work with. We can learn more about ourselves this way than almost any other method used and identify what makes each of us unique and special whilst feeling the oneness of universal energy.

You might like to wear a pendant made from the wood of the tree or carry some other such token of its energy. Magical heart connections can manifest in all kinds of ways from spiritual to medicinal. Your only part to play is in the giving of your own love to it.

Once recognised on a deeper level, the vibration between your energy and that of your magical tree will reverberate strongly every time you come into contact with one of its kind. The magic of this loving relationship will manifest in many ways, some obvious and others less so. It may be that a particular question was posed and answered for you or that a problem needed solving and a solution has appeared or you could have asked for inspiration and now be flowing with creative juices. Whatever form or forms your relationship takes it will be one you can keep for life. This magical heart won't let you down or abandon you, it won't lie to you or hurt you deliberately, it won't upset you or break its promises as it is a heart you can depend on for as long as trees continue to breath so your magical heart will beat. The magical link between the ancient knowledge of the tree and our own inner light deals in honesty and truth so be aware of this when you open up to its energy. There may be issues you have tried to bury or are failing to act positively about and these maybe confronted whilst communing with this inner magic. Some people come face to face with their fears through it and in so doing are given whatever they need in the form of strength, confidence, knowledge and understanding in order to overcome any that are deeply held on to. Trusting in this heart will enable you to cope with dignity with most things life throws your way, safe in the knowledge that all difficulties eventually pass and what may feel like the blackest of holes rarely lasts.

Trees lift spirits so lift your magical heart up to them and give thanks for their beauty and wisdom. In so doing you can feel the mutual euphoria and bathe in the true ecstasy of divine love.

AN EXPERIMENT

Method

First find a willing friend or several and make your way to a local park or woodland. It doesn't matter what time of year or day it is.

Locate a fairly large tree of any type. (If your friend/s are drawn to one in particular then use this one.)

Stand as far as you can from the tree with a clear passage between you and it. (Check for any obstacles such as stones, brambles etc.)

Blindfold your first or only volunteer.

Turn them around five times but make sure they are facing the tree, don't inform them of this though.

Now instruct them to walk and ask them to stop when they believe they are close to a tree.

Take care to stop anyone from actually walking into the tree!

Reaction

Once they are happy that they have reached their destination remove the blindfold.

Take a note of their distance from the tree and mark it in some way. Repeat this three times.

Result

As a rule those who stop far short are probably just a tad fearful and may need to sit with the tree for a while to connect with its energy

Those who stop at the point of the outermost branches are probably very in tune with the tree and have picked up on its aura.

Any who almost walk into the tree are brave but not really feeling the energy of the tree and could do with slowing down.

This exercise is fun and can be a great way to introduce the willing initiate or young to feeling the energy of trees.

Another fun way to feel the heart of a tree is similar and involves blindfolds yet again but this time you walk your friend up to several different trees (thorny ones are best avoided) and just touch them feeling the bark only. They can use their sense of smell also by sniffing their fingers after touching them. This time we are after individual tree identification. But don't help them just let them say everything that comes to mind whilst touching and write down their responses for them to contemplate afterwards.

We are so used to relying on our visual sense initially that it is good sometimes to strengthen our other senses and therefore open up to different levels of communication with the trees.

Remembering that trees don't have eyes in the way we know them but they can see so much.

The Landscape Laughs in Spring
   A sonnet by John Clare 1793–1864

The landscape laughs in Spring and stretches on
Its growing distance of refreshing dyes.
From pewit-haunted flats the floods are gone
And like a carpet the green meadow lies
In merry hues and edged wi' yellow flowers.
The trickling brook veins sparkling to the sun
Like to young may-flies dancing wi' the hours.
The noising children 'mid the young grass run,
Gathering wi' village dames from balk and lea
The swarming cowslips wi' commingling play
To make praise-worthy wine and savoury tea,
And drink a Winter memory of May
When all the season's joys have ceased to be
And flowers and sunny hours have passed away.

4

The Green Man in Literature

The following pages are several stories that I feel have a Green Man influence. Some are traditional tales re-told in my words and briefly examined from his perspective. There may well be many others not included that spring to your mind and if so I apologise in advance for not being aware of them during my time writing this book.

Only one tale is original but was one of my first inspirations when beginning to tackle this mountain so I've bravely put it forward with these other great stories.

I hope you enjoy reading them and don't object to the modern twists I've incorporated at times.

PETER PAN

We are going on a journey to a timeless world where anything is possible and everything that can happen will. This strange and wonderful place is full of adventure and new experiences. It beckons us when we are young and inhabits every wild and unkempt corner. It visits us at night in many weird and unnatural shapes. Sometimes terrifying, sometimes caring, and often just excited, it eventually calls us to rest in its presence.

We will start in early spring as he emerges fresh and bright ready to bring the sparkle back into our eyes. As the young Pan, he is chasing his shadow, anxious to see where it goes and constantly stimulated by its ever-varied changes of direction. Darting first here then there, we see his energy burst forth in early blossom and new buds on trees.

Full of innocent hope and belief in himself he calls his consorts to join him in his great new adventure. Jumping through bedroom windows left ajar, he wakes the young souls sleeping out of their slumber. Cheeky and cocky he crows with delight as the beautiful maiden looks his way. Fluffing himself up he puts on his best lit face and green, vibrating with pure unopposed energy. Now travel with him past the second star on the right until morning to a fairie land of lost souls, shamans and danger.

Let your imagination run and soon the food is real and flying is the ultimate in travel.

Play, tease, be mischievous for this is to be encouraged. Give true love and all is revealed. As spring strengthens it is time to visit the wise ones and see their late exuberance show through the mist or fog of your creation. Connect on a deep level with this new world by dance and song but be aware this situation doesn't last long, for now is the time for war. The energy has worked its way up into a frenzy and sacrifices must be made as each bright spark reaches for its own piece of heaven.

Pan has his enemies too. We are they and he is us. A fierce and impossible dictator and suppresser of souls waits for his battle to commence. The weakness evident has been artificially rectified and is worn upon his arm in defiance of abdication. Pan the brave steps forward to face his death. Death the only true adventure – the greatest of all in the eyes of Pan's enemy. Don't accept it, fight it, and in so doing live with every pore of your being. As Pan does. Swords flash, fists clash and cowards dash away. The fight of inevitability· the only real fight. Pan rises to the challenge unhindered by the opposition in all its glory. Not impressed with the ammunition now stacked against him he cuts through expensive silk with aplomb. Proud and valiant, he jumps first this way then that, ducking and diving, avoiding the steel blade that continues towards him relentlessly until at last the final pitch. Pan wins and raises his sword ready to fight another day. Now racing away from this place of violence he takes us back to the safe and calm of his wild wood. Fairies dart like slithers of silver lace blown in the breeze, pixies throw nuts from high in the trees, elves trip us on branches as we walk as we head for the heart of his sacred space. Our mother, Wendy, awaits and loves us all, embracing her children like a nanny to the world. Her season is about to begin as she is ready for you to harvest her rewards. With gentle caresses and secure embraces she speaks the softly spoken words of love. Far away across the void a bell tolls, just a distant memory of time and space, but we are oblivious to it. Relaxed in the early evening of summer, resting by weeping willows and sparkling rivers. Entranced by moonlight and safe in the knowledge that all is as it should be and always will be.

This peculiar rendition of the popular children's story of Peter Pan came to me after he was mentioned no less than three times in one day by several different people and I felt this was pertinent. The story of Peter Pan and Never Never Land is the story of the young Green Man. Always a boy and yet also a man, he encompasses both aspects of his time and yet remains a creature of all seasons. Facing death as the last great adventure he tells us not to fear it but fight it then face it with dignity when it calls, for it is only a door to another world and this world is infinite. All times are relevant and yet all time is suspended in his world. Peter Pan is a fantastic introduction to the world of the Green Man for any child to encounter. He is rebellious, independent, relies on his wits, lives life to the full and is confident – just as we all are when young. And like every child he longs for a mother who will read him stories and tuck him in at night. He needs loving and this is something we all relate to. The story paints exactly the picture we face today in this world of greed and suppression where nature itself is now under attack by our careless actions.

THE WIND IN THE WILLOWS

Not everyone wants this extreme Green Man in their lives and some prefer a more gentle version.

We begin underground digging upwards, blind. The fresh spring air beckons us out of our winter sleep and we find ourselves on the river bank. A rat scuttles in and out of his home, now flooding under high spring water. We can take our time in the sunshine and admire the comings and goings of this magical place. An otter swims by minding his own business. To us this is all new and stunningly beautiful but we fight against the time and fret over useless chores. The rat slows us down and shares his cunning and survival amongst the reeds and willow trees. We take to the river in his tiny boat and enjoy watching the ducks a-dabbling before resting for the night. Each day is full of new discoveries and friends to be made but constant fear prevails from the wild wood that only the true brave souls dare enter. Danger we are told lurks behind every bush and tree. Only the wise badger dares venture unprotected into its black void.

We meet Toad, who lives in his great mansion, and are bemused by his attraction to humanised consumerism and his self-destructive urge to experiment. We journey with him and delve into his world of crazy ventures and subterfuge. In this place we meet our reflection and are made aware of that which is transient and unfulfilling. He is restrained and yet escapes just like our extreme interference in nature he suffers the endless consequences of his actions until eventually for his own good he is held under house arrest. Unstoppable Toad eventually meets his match with the creatures of the wild wood, or nature itself, as they lay siege to his home and only the friends he deserted can save him from himself. Reluctantly they step in and yet another war is fought.

We, mortals, survive but only just and many fall in this last battle.

The story covers all seasons and explores our relationship from a more complex viewpoint than Peter Pan does. *The Wind in the Willows* is a story of our direct actions on his environment and our reluctance to listen to the message. He steps in at the last moment, much like he is doing now, to save us from ourselves. Toad represents non-harmonists or modern day consumers and his friends are the harmonisers; the creatures of the wild wood are our primal fears and, yes, death yet again.

The eternal cycle.

ROBIN HOOD

We are deep in winter and the snow lays in clumps and drifts across deserted fields. A castle looms in the distance, stone, cold, grey and bleak, it offers us our only chance of rest.

We approach it cautiously for a new king reigns, an impostor at large in his community, hell bent on total control and inducing fear in all he meets. The cold easterly wind shows no mercy as it bites through our tattered garments. We are war-weary and bruised to the bone, hungry and tired, in need of rest. We enter with others trading wares on this unforgiving day. But this is no place for us and we are soon dispatched beyond its walls, running for our lives. We run to the woods and seek solace amongst the thick undergrowth. Hidden from view by tall trees we hide until danger has passed.

As spring melts the snow and streams of water trickle, we hunt for food and build shelters in which to live undisturbed by our enemies. Out of desperation and necessity we rob from the rich and give to the poor. We are outlaws, out of reach and unconventional. We give generously and bide our time. As May approaches we dance and sing, calling love in her name, and to our surprise a maiden comes our way. A spellbound Robin takes one look at his lady and knows her heart for it is his own. She, embarrassed by his brazen glances, turns away. They journey deep into the sacred space protected by the spirit of the woods. As night falls food is shared and the young Robin sings to his maid a song of love and longing. She is caught in the moment, held suspended in time as his magic weaves its way through her veins, and love for this man beats strong under her ribs. They know instantly of their fate but faint heart never won fair maiden and soon he discovers this to be true. Almost as soon as they first meet he loses her back to her normal life in the castle keep. Held there against her will as bait by the usurper to the true king's throne to lure young Robin out of hiding, she waits petrified with fear. Fear for him, his friends and herself.

Robin wins the day, of course, through genius and wins the hand of his lady just as the true king returns jubilant from battle.

The emphasis of the life spent in the woods foraging is a tale not uncommon to our friend the Green Man and this adult aspect of his story is the basis for most of his message. He rebukes riches and fights a war on slavery and poverty, helping preserve life underground throughout winter. In spring he meets his maid and they fall in love just as nature itself is at this time. By summer they are fighting a battle for the harvest to come and having to rely on trust and faith and belief to win the day. At the end of summer and into autumn they prepare for winter once again and rest briefly before embarking upon yet another season. The story reflects the adult world of responsibility and romantic love connected with the expectations of each season.

The dark and menacing aspect represented by the greedy Prince John and his sheriff represent that which we must overcome in order to win our battles in life and remind us that love and justice are worth fighting for.

The connection between this legendary character and Sherwood Forest goes far deeper into our past than we can really imagine. If it were possible that a race of indigenous Britons lived in these great forests well before modern humans made it out of Africa then we have a different story. The meeting of these two differently evolved peoples must have caused a reaction and may have led to the many fears of wild woodsmen or 'bogey men'. Taking this concept through time, well after the initial meetings and deep into the dark ages, we may well have an answer to how a character called Robin came about. By now any indigenous Britons would be extinct or else we would have evidence of their lives, which as far as I know we don't. But the necessary skills for surviving in woodland would be intact and the myths and legends of these extinct creatures abound. Imagine for a moment that you are a young lad trying desperately to survive in a small poverty stricken village. Your family are starving, as are you, and the penalty for helping yourself to nature's banquet is death. In this extreme but all too common case what would you do?

Poach, obviously, what else. You would hope not to get caught but what if you were? Would you try to escape punishment or face the music? A dilemma with potentially far reaching consequences. Or could you take your chances in the wild wood and every now and then secretly deliver food to your family's doorstep in the night? Possibly. So you see how it might have evolved, then again you might not have been so magnanimous or your family could be punished for your illegal actions. This Robin Hood/Green Man is simply nature and man surviving together and working together in mutual harmony.

RED RIDING HOOD

As the people of the village sleep a baby cries out for its mother deep in the woods nearby. Unheard by any people the baby whimpers plaintively, resting in its swaddling under the boughs of a large ash tree. Warm breath wafts over his face and a gentle tongue licks his fingers before teeth firmly grip the swaddling and carry the child off into the night.

FIFTEEN YEARS LATER

The carpenter's daughter spends a restless night disturbed by the desires of her dream – the dream that keeps coming, again and again. She is running through the woods and hounds from the village chase her with angry villagers shouting curses. Faster and harder she runs, deeper and deeper into the dark shadows of the night, until exhausted she can run no more and collapses under a large tree. Fear penetrates every pore and although she is tired her senses are still alert to every sound and smell around her. All has gone quiet; no longer pursued, she surrenders to the creatures of the night and seeks solace in the occasional hoot of an owl and timid approach of a curious deer. But still the fear persists as she is alone and vulnerable, thrown to the mercy of the wolves. One howls and her spine tingles but she cannot move: her legs have become roots buried down in the soil around her. She can hear their feet thundering closer and almost smell their breath under her nose but still she remains stuck.

Then she wakes.

Every month the same dream and yet it made little or no sense to the girl who was by all accounts a good girl and well liked and respected by her family. On the evening before the harvest moon a young man came from the next village, so he said, over the great river. He came with news of a feast being held and the invitation was for all of the carpenter's people. Cautiously the offer was accepted and the young man was invited to eat with the carpenter's family that night. He was an unusual chap and, although his manner and dress were quite different to any they knew, the young girl was surprised by his accepted status within their community. He told a sad tale of his village and how many years ago a baby had gone missing, presumed taken by wolves, and how at full moon this child's cries could be heard carried by the wind.

The carpenter's daughter listened entranced by the raw beauty of this lean fellow and totally mesmerised by his full eyes and watchful gaze. Her heart beat faster as he glanced her way, giving her a knowing smile as he did. She equated the fear from her dream related to this feeling and she was upset and confused but tried hard to conceal it.

Once finished with eating the young man thanked them for their hospitality and went on his way.

That night she had the dream again.

The next day she was sent on an errand to visit her grandmother but warned as per usual not to stray from the path and to be back before night fall. The girl donned her cloak and skipped off into the woods glad to be free of her normal chores for the day.

The late summer heat felt suffocating and the air was hard to breath so she took her time picking flowers along the way. Suddenly she realised she'd lost her way and didn't recognise any of the trees or deer tracks around her. Darkness enveloped her and a mist began to rise all around. Panicking she started to run, but where to? As she ran faster and harder blindly into the trees she dropped her basket without even noticing. Eventually, exhausted and out of breath, she sat down under a large ash tree asking it to protect her from harm. Crying self-piteously she fell asleep.

Several hours later she began to wake as a strange wet sensation drew her attention to her feet. Rubbing her eyes to try to focus, she just made out what looked like many pairs of yellow eyes staring back at her. As her eyes cleared she froze in fear at the sight of a pack of wolves encircling her tree. All except one crouched down around her tree but the one licking her feet continued. She gasped and he stopped, looking up into her eyes. As their eyes met her heart jumped a beat and she backed into the bark of the tree as hard as she could, wishing it would swallow her into its bark but to no avail. Unlike the other wolves this one had human eyes, big blue ones, his nose looked different too, as did his mouth, and slowly she began to see the face of the young man who had visited their house the previous night.

A fierce heat grew inside her and as fear subsided desire took its place, a desire of such intensity and so primal it shook her to the very core. So beautiful his eyes, so firm his limbs, so handsome and tempting yet.... She could hear the villagers' curses and feel the rejection of her family if she were to allow this man to take her.

Frustrated and confused she let out a blood curdling scream and heard instead an echoed howl return. Gently he reached out for her hands and she surrendered to his arms in deep embrace. Unperturbed by his pack and oblivious to the danger she gave herself to the young man under the blood red harvest moon. As their two became one she filled with passion and an energy released through her body she now realised she'd only ever experienced asleep.

After some time they fell asleep wrapped in each other, arms and legs linked together nestling into each other's faces as love flowed between them like the gentle flow of the great river in summer.

As she awoke next morning she found herself alone under the tree but could hear the sound of voices calling her name far off in the distance. She looked around for her young man but couldn't see him. Her cloak lay torn under her and her clothes were in tatters all about. A trickle of blood ran down the inside of her legs and ashamed she did her best to remove it.

The villagers grew closer and she called to them. Eventually they found her and her father rushed over shocked at the state of his daughter in her ragged clothes, leaves stuck in her hair and scratches like giant claw marks down her back.

'Wolves did this to my daughter' he announced.

She tried to say different but couldn't speak so they carried her home.

'Grandma' she managed to say.

'Your grandmother died last night' her mother sobbed. They had found her that morning whilst searching for the young girl.

'How did she die?' the young girl asked sobbing at the news.

'In her sleep dear, naturally' her mother answered.

That night they hunted the wolves and the carpenter's daughter lay tormented with guilt in her bed unable to do a thing. The sound of a baby echoed in her head and the frightened face of her young man appeared in her mind's eye.

It was his fear she felt in the dream.

Her fear too.

By midnight she could take it no more and crept out into the woods to find him.

They never saw her again but found her cloak hanging from a large ash in the middle of the woods.

This highly peculiar rendition of Little Red Riding Hood by any account could resonate with many young women as they go through the trials and tribulations of puberty. During this 'dark age' we are confronted by our own inner sexual 'wyrd' and discover much about our primal selves. Very little is talked about it or written and yet this remains a crucial initiation for all. As new hormones rush through our veins we experience strong sexual desires, natural but considered dangerous. We are warned not to stray off the path by our elders and to conform to society's expectations in our potential lovemaking. As the beast within rises we are cautious of responding to its call, for to do so in complete abandonment is 'off the path'. So we fight it, night after night ignoring its energy, feeling the fire burn but having no outlet for it.

Masturbation is suppressed and still to this day has stigma placed upon it. Its OK for boys — they can't help themselves — but not totally accepted for girls. So what does a girl do when faced with the true wild untameable nature of her desire? Well if she stays on the path she will never know but I'd get off it if I were you, girls!

PERSONAL INSPIRATION

Back in mid-spring around the time of Easter I visited a part of Thetford Forest for some inspiration. Although most of this once great deciduous wood is now forestry controlled sustainable pine lined up in rows like soldiers it still has some special spots. It was to one such place I ventured and felt drawn into a clump of young trees about seven feet high. Surprised but intrigued I followed my nose, as it were, until I came upon a natural clearing in which stood a young holly and equally young oak.

'Oh wow' I remember thinking and felt instantly grateful too.

I sat here for a while and tuned into the energy of the space. It felt full of hope and promise. Once home again I hoped some inspiration would arrive and by evening it had. I had a tale to tell. A story from the forest and one that may well have happened. This is it.

THE FACE IN THE TREE

As the sun's rays burned through the early morning mist, steam rose from the thatched roof of the woodsman's house on the edge of the copse. My lazy horse, who was always more than happy to gallop away from the keep for the benefit of the king, now plodded towards the clearing as if it were nothing but my sheer cruelty that kept us together. 'Bless him' I thought drawing back on the thick leather reins to grind him to an obliging halt in front of Jane, the woodsman's wife.

'What can we do for a king's man?' she asked, holding the eggs she'd gathered up in her apron and gesturing to her daughter to come close.

Pretending to read from the scroll given to me I answered her,

'The king requests five tall straight mature oaks of at least fifty foot be felled in his name by your husband, Edmund, for the building of a new church in the village of Felham. He must bring them to the village green for inspection by the priest and the king himself.'

'Huh, does he indeed', retorted the now disgruntled woman who turned her back towards the house in disgust at my instructions.

'To ignore this command will be folly madam', I quickly retorted whilst dismounting and tying my horse to a nearby tree.

She quickly asked her young child to get a basket for her fragile cargo and I watched as they slowly and deliberately placed the eggs in the clean straw lining. At the age of thirty Jane was unusual in that she had two children born so far apart but the advantages were clear to me. Edmund her husband had his tall strong son to help him in his work and now Jane, who still looked good for her age with her ruddy round cheeks and upturned nose, had her pretty, fair young daughter to assist around the home.

'Edmund has only just started cutting the copse today and now you want him to stop his work and fell great trees. This will need a great many hands. Has the king thought of that, I ask you?' Jane stood with her back to the house, arms resting on her generous hips, in defiance of my message.

My horse's bridle had become tangled in bramble and while I bent down to try and release the beast I answered 'The king said you'd say that and his answer is this. This is God's work and many hands will be sent to help you. Your family will be well rewarded for their efforts once the job is done, have no fear.'

Her daughter, Daisy, collected an armful of hay from the tiny barn doorway, careful not to touch the main supply, and dodging the puddles came over shyly to feed my stubborn mount.

Jane looked deep in thought, her hand on her chin. Then she beckoned me into her home out of the crisp autumn air.

The house had been built by her father-in-law many moons ago and, although he had long passed on, his legacy remained as a testament to his goodly craftsmanship. Intricate carving wove its way around the doorframe and the familiar smell of burning charcoal wafted out as I ducked my head to enter.

The single room had been sectioned by poles and wattle to provide the family with three separate bedchambers on the right, and to the left stood a large oak table and two benches. Sides of smoked meat hung from the high vaulted ceiling, as did bundles of the many varied herbs Jane used for her infusions.

A small trunk occupied the far side with a platter of freshly baked flat breads on top of it. They had been griddled that morning on a flat pan under the cauldron that hung from its great iron hook over the hearth. Vegetable and rabbit pottage bubbled away, gently filling the room with gastronomic anticipation fuelled by its aroma.

She was a good woman as was her husband, and much like the rest of their community; they led a simple but physically demanding life. Jane was well respected by her peers, and by the king, as both the local midwife and herbalist: indeed his own children had been delivered by her. Out of mutual respect their families had co-existed for many generations and the king had indeed been generous to them over the years, increasing their land allowance, even going to the lengths of providing food out of his own stores when times grew hard.

I sat down on the little rustic stool offered and admired their cosy dwelling enjoying the comfort of warmth and homeliness it offered me albeit briefly.

Jane, still silent, poured a mug of ale and handed it to me to drink, I thanked her for her kindness and asked her for a reply to the king's order.

'I will speak with my husband upon his return, that is all I can say', she eventually answered with an air of annoyance.

'Perhaps madam I have been unclear in my message. This is not a request but a direct order and I must return with news of your compliance', I replied kindly but firmly.

'I cannot know my husband's mind and therefore cannot answer on his behalf', she said picking up her besom and brushing the leaves back out of the door that Daisy had left open upon her return.

'Then I will speak with him', I said reluctantly getting up, having hoped she would agree on his behalf, and save me the trouble of persuading my horse to travel the heavy ploughed land between their cottage and the copse.

Thanking her kindly I agreed, after much pestering, to take Daisy with me to visit her father and brother in the woods. Jane lifted the child up in front of me and we set off slowly, my mount having decided the extra weight reduced his speed to nothing greater than a medium walk.

In virtual secrecy Edmund's family still followed the old ways and hung on to many of their beliefs. Yesterday they had enjoyed a feast in remembrance of the ancestors, and now the old year had died it was time to get on with the new one.

This was an important day on the calendar and respect was shown to the spirit of the forest before they began. Edmund had taken extra food and ale with him to offer this being and had lovingly placed it in the stool of the first tree they cut. Peter their son was coming on well at learning his trade and had now mastered both felling and splitting the hazel, making his arthritic father's work a little easier. Whilst Edmund stacked brush into hedging to protect the cut area from deer and boar that would eat the young shoots once they sprouted forth, Peter sang his cutting song as he rhythmically swung his treasured billhook up and down.

It had been a cold morning but the early mist had soon cleared to produce a clear and radiant day with the copse glistening a myriad of autumnal colours. At midmorning, or thereabouts, they stopped their work to sit in front of the fire and eat. The clearing they sat in would become the spiritual heart of their working lives for the rest of the season. In this space they would spend their winter cutting, sorting, splitting wood for hurdle making amongst many other crafts besides. Any leftover wood could be either bundled into faggots for burning or turned into charcoal to sell in the market in the spring. Peter was keen to learn all his father's trade and this summer they would be making besoms, so birch tops were being collected and set aside for this purpose. Cutting clumps of birch cleared spaces in which the deer would gather to graze, rut and eventually in June give birth. There was always something new to learn and Edmund was a kind and patient father who did his best to encourage Peter.

My arrival shattered their silence and caused the robin availing himself of crumbs dropped by the pair to fly off.

'Father look at me', Daisy called from aloft.

Stiffly Edmund stood tall and reached for his excited offspring who grudgingly let go of the clump of mane she'd been clinging on to and hugged his broad shoulders as he let her down.

'Has some ill befallen your mother, child?', he asked, surprised at the scene now in front of him. It wasn't every day a messenger of the king delivered his daughter to him.

'No father, I just wanted a ride', she answered in a flippant manner.

'So then, what brings you here man?'

I repeated my order from the king and as expected it was met with a frown from the woodsman. The promise of many hands to help him was met with better a response, though, and after much deliberation and consultation with Peter his son they agreed.

Later that day Edmund, Peter and Daisy returned home to discuss the issue with Jane over dinner. Jane ladled portions of pottage out into four wooden bowls and called Peter, who was checking their pigs.

'What do you make of today then wife?' Edmund said through his food and winking at his daughter who swung her legs and smiled mischievously back at her father.

'Oh I suppose we knew it would happen. Every other village has a church. I just wish the king had seen fit to give us more warning', Jane answered as Peter entered.

'Well I for one just hope this lad they are sending me is up to the work', their son commented before sitting down to enjoy his supper.

'And I hope we all are son', Edmund replied between mouthfuls.

'The money will surely come in useful', Jane said, reaching over for more bread to pass to her hungry family, 'We could do with some new ironware and I was thinking about getting a horse to make your work easier. Now we have the top paddock it could live there with the sheep', she suggested as Daisy started jumping up and down with excitement.

'Oh could we now', Edmund answered, knowing only too well the corner he was backed into by them all.

'So the king wants his church, you want this horse and all I want is an easy life. Well I suppose I'd better do it and keep you all happy but you better pray to this new God for fair weather', Edmund said picking up his giggling daughter and putting her to bed for the night.

'I'll be off too', their son said kissing them both goodnight.

'I love you wife.'

'I love you husband'. Edmund and Jane embraced before tidying up for the night.

Then they spent a quiet hour or so together, Jane sewing up Edmund's boots and Edmund whittling a piece of wood he had secreted in his pouch, before eventually they both collapsed into a restful sleep.

The following evening after packing away their tools and tidying the 'work area' Peter left early and Edmund was alone to wander the edge of the great forest next to the copse.

As Edmund trod the grass path between the plough and the tree line with the sun setting behind him he noticed the light catch what appeared to be a face staring down from a large oak tree. The deep orange of the setting sun lit up this manifestation dramatically and indeed, as Edmund stood focused on it, features began to appear.

Its eyes were like black jet and the mouth seemed half open as if in speech. The air grew chilly and all around stillness pervaded. The face became more defined with every second Edmund looked at it. An owl swooped down low past him into the grass and he could hear the deer rutting in the distance.

Worried that this might be a sign from the old ones that he should disobey the king's order, he knelt out of respect under the great tree, its limbs almost touching the ground in places as it stretched in competition from the others of its kind around it. Every shade of green, yellow and brown were displayed upon its leaves and acorns lay about on the ground waiting to be eaten by opportunistic creatures of the impending night.

'Great Oak tree listen to my plea', he started. 'The king demands five oaks and that I make him a church for the village of Felham. If I refuse he will punish my family and they will all suffer. What can I do but agree?' he pleaded.

Edmund stared intently at the face and heard nothing but the wind slowly the leaves began to fall and as they did he heard a voice, almost a whisper on the breeze,

> *'It matters not, not a jot,*
> *It matters not, to me.*
> *Be who you are, with me,*
> *With me, you will be free.'*

Taking heed of these magical words and watching the leaves as they fell almost deliberately to the forest floor Edmund now noticed the other five tall straight oak trees that encircled his vociferous one.

Uplifted and absolved Edmund took it as a sign that the forest was happy with making a sacrifice on behalf of the 'new religion' and forgetting his arthritic knees for a few minutes skipped home like a young stag.

Many weeks passed and on behalf of the king I was asked to keep an eye on the progress Edmund and his motley crew made. Edmund instructed his help sent from the keep now assembled to cut only the five trees around the one with the face. To cut a tree such as this was still seen as bad luck so they took great care not to disturb it too much when felling the others. Peter took over his father's work, aided by a lad sent to him from the village, eager to learn the trade and assist in any way he could.

Once felled and cleared the great oak stood alone, proud of his newly acquired status and keen to stretch his branches in the early evening light. Edmund hung back from the others as they left for the evening and drew a small wooden carving he'd whittled the night before from out of the small leather pouch that hung from his belt. It was a giant acorn beautifully and lovingly carved and about five times the size of a natural one that he placed respectfully among the roots. Sensing the tree's response he looked up at the face and was relieved to see it almost appearing to grin down at him. Then almost without any conscious thought Edmund began to plant all the acorns he found around the perimeter of the great oak's branches.

Once done with his impulsion he walked back fairly briskly home to the warmth and love of his family who were anxious to hear how his day had gone. He told them they were to be sent a team of oxen the next day to haul the great trunks to Felham and Edmund was secretly looking forward to his dubious task of overseeing the job.

In truth Edmund enjoyed his work and took great pride, as he always did, in always doing his best and it was for that reason the king had chosen him for this holy work.

Five weeks to the day later and just before the winter solstice Edmund rose early. It was still dark outside but the moon's light was casting long shadows inside their home. Unable to return to sleep, Edmund decided to make an early start and trying carefully not to disturb the others he got up.

His wife groaned and turned over, but Daisy heard him and sat up to peer through her curtain at her father putting on his boots.

'Where are you going father?' she asked in her whispered voice.

'I'm just off to the church my love. Go back to sleep', he answered smiling at her in the semi-darkness.

By the time he had travelled the two miles to the green, dawn was breaking and a cacophony of cockerels could be heard crowing from all directions. Ahead he could clearly make out the imposing sight of his great skeleton standing alone on its platform of green grass.

He smiled to himself at his work; yes he was proud, why shouldn't he be? He thought. The split and smoothed off beams with their perfectly honed joints would last, he observed, longer than they would have done if left growing in such close proximity to each other in the forest.

Magically a face appeared amongst the knots and whorls he planed towards as he sat astride this last great beam. It would be placed across the entrance to the church once finished for all to see as they entered the church. This face had a feminine grace to it unlike the essentially masculine one on the great oak in the forest. Instinctively he stopped working and allowed himself to be temporarily entranced by its elusive beauty. As he did so, the wind picked up just a touch and Edmund listened; a voice as beautiful as any nightingale could be heard singing:

> *'This face you see is me,*
> *I know you and you me*
> *Forever eternally'.*

Then just as had happened in the woods when he planted the acorns, he began automatically and without much thought to carve out the features. By the time dawn had properly broken his crew of willing assistants arrived. They were shocked and stunned by the vista that greeted them. Edmund stood up humbly and concerned at their response but stood his ground in spite of their pleas to remove it before the king and his new priest arrived that midday.

Undeterred, Edmund finished polishing the beam and between them they lifted it into its final resting place.

'On your head be it', his right-hand man Gavin said as the king approached.

'What magnificent work Edmund!' the king proclaimed at first sight of this imposing structure.

'A true house of God' the priest confirmed.

Then they saw it.

High above the entrance, a face of such divine elegance emerging from a sea of leaves smiling beneficently down upon them.

'What's this?' the king asked Edmund, looking the woodsman straight in the eye as he dismounted from his shining black steed.

At the back of the group I groaned inwardly as I saw Edmund's handiwork in all its glory.

'Hold my horse man', the king instructed me and I too descended to ground level to hold the two beasts.

'Such craftsmanship, what delicate features, I have never seen the like', the priest observed. All eyes and ears, including the now silent king's, were upon the holy man as he stepped forward to inspect the face more closely.

'Why God himself must have guided your hand in this; we will leave it be as a testament to our craftsman for his love and honour of our church', he declared and we all sighed with relief, not least Edmund who, I must admit, was trembling by now.

And so it was, and is, and will be forever, a testament of love.

Years went by and Edmund eventually passed away leaving his elderly widow, her son and his new family to continue living and working in the copse. Daisy left home to marry the priest's son and the king kindly granted me a cottage in which to see out my twilight years. I visit Jane often and many a time we walk down to the great oak with her grandchildren and enjoy telling them the story of their grandfather and the tree face in the church. The trunk has thickened and knurled and the canopy of branches has widened, making it the grandest of trees on that edge of the forest.

On one such day this Easter past, her eldest grandchild Lewis exclaimed as the others ran around the circle of young oaks and bluebells that now grow around this great old tree, 'Look grandma, look Bevan, there's a face, look everyone up there in the tree'. We looked up and sure enough there it was Edmund's tree face, as it always had been, grinning down on us from on high benevolently.

Or as the seventeenth century poet Andrew Marvell put it in his poem 'The Garden'.

A great deal of poetic licence was used in the creation of this story and I hope this is accepted. In truth oak requires some time to 'season' or dry out before it can be used.

> *No white nor red was ever seen*
> *So am'rous as this lovely green*
> *Fond lovers, cruel as their flame*
> *Cut in these Trees their Mistress name*
> *Little Alas they know or heed*
> *How far these beauties hers exceed*
> *Fair Trees! Where s'eer your barkes I wound*
> *No name shall but your own be found*

THE GREEN KNIGHT

Tommy Prince held the gang together – without him their individual weaknesses would show. The 'Wheel Gang' were honest, brave and true to each other but lethal to any who crossed their path with fighting on their minds. This day found them celebrating a post-Christmas binge of presents and cake and cider they'd nicked from Dave's dad's beer cellar at the Rose and Crown. Their secret den lay deep in a disused quarry cunningly disguised as an old shed. Inside it was Arthur's court and they were the Knights of the wobbly round wire bobbin table. Behind the shed lay their trusty steeds, twelve shiny new stunt bikes yet to be put through their paces on the assault course crudely created outside from planks and artificially moulded mounds of earth. The showing off and boasting carried on well after dark and soon the lads talked of the girls they had their beady eyes on but all were envious of Tommy for he held a gem in his hands – the lovely Aveline. Dave squirmed uncomfortably, knowing only too well the sordid and lustful thoughts that many held for her but he bit his tongue and joined in regardless. A small fire made from sticks and newspaper was lit in the grate as darkness fell and Tommy rose to ignite the old gas lamp he'd proudly repaired for their use.

Soon talk of dares and practical jokes they played upon the other gangs arose in conversation and all trembled slightly inside as they awaited Tommy's customary challenge. Who would it be this time? They all pondered, trying to keep the laughs going and avoid tempting Tommy into action for once he dared, you dared, or risk leaving the gang. No-one questioned Tommy's authority. He would do anything asked of him, no dare was too risky for Tommy – his bravery was legendary.

Then just as Tommy rose to throw down his first gauntlet a terrible noise was heard from outside the door. They all jumped sideways, little Sam the terrier yelping as Dave sat down on his tail.

The door crashed open and in came a young man on his bike. No ordinary young man for this one was dressed from head to toe in green.

'Ho!' he shouted as they tried to take in this arboreal vision before them. Upon his head a mop of green hair trailing down his back with ivy twisted as if still growing out of his scalp, his very skin tainted lichen green and emerald his twinkling eyes.

His clothes were covered in bright shiny jewels like diamonds sparkling on a velvet cushion. His boots were made of top quality leather, green naturally, and had holly leaves imprinted on the left boot and an axe on the right. The Green Knight had such presence and manner that our friends were temporarily silenced in awe of this apparition. He was the size of three of them rolled together but didn't seem threatening, which confused them.

'Who is in charge here?' he asked, staring around the room.

Silence pervaded until at last Tommy came forward.

'I am, what do you want?' he bravely inquired, puffing his chest and straightening his back.

'I'm here to check you out, I've been sent by one who rules'.

'Who's that then?' asked Tommy, their illustrious but very nervous leader.

'One whom you cannot as yet meet but he's heard good things about you and asks that you take up his arms', the strange one replied.

Murmurings and twittering buzzed around the old shed with its not so brave knights all crouched low and huddled up against its draughty wooden slatted walls.

Before Tommy could roll up his sleeves Dave stood up and, putting his thin arm across Tommy's thick forearm, he said, 'I'll take you on'.

Tommy looked his friend straight in the eye and tried to talk him out of it but after a quick flare up conceded, for he was never one to stop pure bravery in its tracks.

The green one dismounted from his steed and leant it up in the doorway, blocking the exit. As he turned he drew a knife from his belt.

Quietly and calmly he handed it hilt first to Dave, who by now appeared quite pale, and yet gulping he took it from our Green friend.

'If you can strike me a lethal blow I'll not stop you', he said coolly as a gasp of disbelief went around the room.

Dave hesitated as the young man in green stood firm, smiling unfazed by the potential harm coming his way.

'Strike boy, strike me, I'll not move a muscle, you have my word', he encouraged the reticent Dave.

Dave held the knife high above his head and swung from right to left across the neck of the stranger. To the shock and horror of all who saw the knife cut clean through his throat like butter and the Green Man's head rolled to the floor. Terrified, the Wheel Gang shook, unable to move. They were all paralysed with fear.

Dave let the blade fall and its clang resounded around the now silent room.

Undeterred by his decapitated state the Green Knight walked over towards Tommy and bent down to pick up his head.

Carefully he placed it back upon his shoulders and then to all their horror and amazement spoke. 'Now the challenge is yours, to seek me out next year and meet your destiny'.

The gang shook and trembled, some having trouble containing the contents of their churning stomachs.

Without more ado the knight re-mounted his bike and rode off into the night.

Tommy held Dave in his arms like a father comforting his child and the rest of the gang sat staring at him waiting for him to say something, anything.

'I don't know if what just happened was real', he started, knowing he had to come up with something to reassure his motley crew, 'but I do know this, that was no man or boy – that, my friends, was a ghost and I think we just had ourselves a haunting'.

Sighs of relief spread round the shed and gradually they talked of the sighting and told tales of other ghostly happenings and soon they were laughing again.

Tommy decided it was time for them to leave and as they put out the fire and the light Dave stammered, 'but what about this?' holding up the Green Knight's knife still dripping with his blood.

'Keep it', Tommy said leaning towards his shaking mate, 'we may have need of that next year'.

This modern day interpretation of the legend of the Green Knight from the tales of King Arthur and the Knights of the Round Table could resound with all young people today. Gangs are becoming more prolific and although born out of boredom they frequently indulge in the old initiations and tests much as Arthur's Knights were supposed to have done. Pride in bravery, strength, skills and unity keep these tribes together. In the supposed time of Arthur many tribes and kings ruled, each fighting for their piece of England's cake much as some gangs do today. But as history repeatedly shows us its not the offensive attackers that win the day but those who instead choose to defend well. We are taught from a young age to believe in love and honour as our strengths but constantly have to defend this belief as there are always those who, through greed for power born out of fear, attempt to destroy all they encounter.

The appearance of the Green Knight was indicative of a time when nature again felt challenged by man's behaviour and sought to send a Knight to show allegiance to the brave and just who would act in his name. The appearance of the Green Knight is acknowledgement of the Knight's ability to face the greatest quest ever and that is the defence of nature herself. Today's spiritual warriors and eco-defenders are also Green Knights challenging every bulldozer, whose path they lay across, to kill them. Tommy's gang could be any one of these eco-warriors as could many of the young people today. Only the bravest warriors are sought by the Green Knight. He isn't interested in those who would flinch from battle but nor is he interested in those who would make battle. He needs people to help defend his realm, youngsters like Tommy and his mates as well as everyone else who would join up to defend the Green Man's right to life.

Tied to trees by rope and chain,
Road builders they are here again

But in the mud and diggers hues
Crusty hippies, amid true blues

Silent vigil by day and night
Resisting, showing great insight
We shouldn't be so bloody keen
To carve up hill and dale between

Through cold night air and rain
The defenders of your earthly reign
Hang on regardless of their plight
Hoping bureaucracy takes flight

The young, the old the caring ones,
Bodies are shields; there are no guns,
Tunnels that stretch far underground
In musty hollows Swampy found

In reverence you duly fight
It keeps you strong in dark and light
Your holy name on every green
Trees are natures exemplars seen

And so to those whose sword is clean
Whose hearts and minds in nature glean
Such majesty and beauty found
Reaching up, from here, the ground.

To you I say, 'train more like you'
To walk in woods and love them too
Embracing natures harmony
Your legacy for all to see!

Mary Neasham 2003

5

His Message Today

I cannot claim to arrogantly 'know' his ultimate, definitive or whole message today but I do feel strongly that buried inside all of us is an inner knowing of the soul of the Green Man. To know his soul is to know ourselves but for many of us this is no easy task as we now choose to detach from nature and stay safe in our centrally heated homes and air conditioned offices. Each generation moves farther away from the rawness of nature's forces and lives in an increasingly protected environment, oblivious to the reality outside. I grew up in London and as a child we didn't have many of the luxuries that are considered the norm today such as wall to wall carpeting and double glazing. When it was frosty outside it was frequently frosty inside but it did us no harm. Even in this great metropolis we felt each season as it arrived. The same cannot be said today. I moved back to the city after an eight year stint in the harsher but energised west country and spent three years rediscovering my roots. My, how they'd changed. A new motorway now carved its way straight through the heart of my home in spite of years of active protest against its intrusion into our lives, at the cost of many houses and a few ancient chestnuts and oaks. This modern dilemma of road building to accommodate our ever-increasing need for more cars is unlikely to be resolved in the immediate future but sympathy for nature is increasing as a result. The most obvious and intriguing change I personally experienced was the detachment from seasonal change. Only drastic weather conditions make any mark on city dwellers. Our parks and trees reflect the true conditions and one only has to look at the state of many city trees to see the pollution damage they try to resist on a daily basis. We are forced to breath unhealthy air and avoid direct contact with green and natural places by living in cities and only the few deliberately venture into the Green Man's true environment. This need and desire to control our space and create a neutral bland grey world of offices, shops, restaurants and other such buildings dampens the soul over time and suppresses our more natural instincts, which have no place in today's modern technological age. Or so it seems. Out of fear, necessity, and survival we have arrived at the point we are today and one could argue that all we have done has been for the greater good of humanity. Yes, we have eradicated many deadly diseases with our modern drugs and lessened the need for pain as a consequence and who can blame us for having the intelligence to overcome such hardships?

But as each virus and bacterium is beaten a new more deadly one seems to pop up in its place. Science thinks genetics hold the key, and in part I'm sure they do, but it's the magical life force that I believe will avoid direct control and therefore constantly elude science in its efforts.

Genetic cloning is an excellent example of our clumsiness. Many people today are becoming increasingly alarmed at the potential future of genetic engineering and fear the creation of a superior race of humans that relegate the rest of us to second-class citizens. I put my trust in nature, though, and am sufficiently happy to believe this won't ever happen. To make this point I refer to the discovery of antibiotics as a much welcomed landmark in medicinal history. Due to our interference and short sightedness we are now faced with 'super bugs' that have evolved by overcoming the methods used to control or destroy them. Nature can prove to us time and time again how adaptable and inscrutable it is from the microcosmic to the macrocosmic level and as these areas are our building blocks of life it follows that to alter one will inevitably influence the whole, one way or another. Holistic science is doing a far better job of understanding these links and patterns by working in harmony rather than attempting to direct healing in one focused spot. In many respects our ancient ancestors also thought they knew better. Modern knowledge of our pre-history shows us as continuously using up our resources and utilising nature's powers to defend ourselves against predators. It is now believed amongst anthropologists that after the retreat of the last ice age our human ancestors with their new stone age 'tools' pillaged the earth so substantially they nearly drove themselves to extinction, along with the many animals they had hunted.

Similarly the ancient nomads of Australia are thought to have increased forest fires in an attempt to destroy the last Jurassic reptilian predator, which in turn altered the landscape considerably from forest to grass land and subsequently increased kangaroo numbers. One of the few ancient races to have learnt their lessons regarding sustainability were the Native Americans who sadly were replaced by the buffalo-hunting 'new Americans' of the nineteenth century. As a race we have a tendency towards using up our resources, something it is believed the emergence of agriculture was trying to redress.

By domesticating animals and growing crops, man took his first step towards sustainability – something we have attempted to continue to this day but something has gone wrong. I feel that the resurgence of interest in the Green Man and nature's spirit generally is due to a deep and primitive ancestral knowledge we all have inside us screaming at us to stop and take notice of the damage we are now inflicting upon the Earth and its ever decreasing resources. This is a commonly held belief, knowing and understanding that what we all share is telling us we are in danger of literally losing the plot.

For many people involved with the Green movement and those still living close to the land this is old news but for those outside such influence it is an unpleasant truth they'd rather not face. Over the past hundred years or so our relationship with nature has changed and much like our ancestors we have shifted many of its natural balances by our well-meant interference. But the answer we all want to know now in our world of technological advances is, 'can we have our cake and eat it?' I believe we can, as do many ecologists and environmentalists, but it will mean a global change in attitude that due to our market-led forces must be implemented by the business world. So it would appear that to achieve a modern redress and improved harmony we have to make it pay. This is a sad reflection of our times, but an honest one, and one those in positions of power today should be taking seriously, especially if they wish to remain in power.

By gaining a spiritual connection with nature at root level we can all take an individual brave step forward and in doing so will invariably feel the need to reflect this in our everyday life. There are many ways we can do this, from drastically changing our shopping habits to more thoughtful and ethical consumerism to involving ourselves in local conservation and environmental issues. This personal adaptation can be difficult, though, and is not helped by the 'fat cats' of modern industry who constantly lure us with delectable treats we cannot possibly do without. For this reason many people are reluctant to change their ways. Although the onus should be on each and every one of us it is not an easy path to tread as many of us have built up dependencies and addictions that we are reluctant and fearful of breaking from. It is also a sad reflection of our western times that to stand outside the accepted 'norm' constitutes extreme behaviour amongst the peer group. It is

increasingly difficult for younger people, especially, to display individua-
listic tendencies. As a child of the sixties, individualism and free expression
was encouraged, perhaps too much, but the pendulum has now swung
the other way and many modern young people in the developed world
today are reluctant to stand alone in any way at all. This flocking
behaviour, of almost total uniformity, can depress the creative side and
suppresses individual thought, creating a generation of sheep all keen to
pay to advertise their allegiance to a particular brand and almost incapable
of imaginative expression. It is also possible for one to imagine that the
individual creative explosion of the postwar world created these resource
needs in the first place and that today's young people are simplifying their
collective needs which could eventually make it easier for governments to
implement the changes now very much required. Our choices are
obvious to me, we are about to enter an increasingly restrictive market
of high technology and increased global awareness, combined with a
future of decreasing resources and infinite re-cycling of those in current
circulation. Our most pressing need is fuel, with the world's current
supply of fossil fuels now diminishing at an alarming rate. Companies
that sell power as a resource must instigate radical changes for our
future if we are to avoid a global man-made catastrophe. So what has
this all to do with the Green Man? Well everything really, as it is most
definitely a large part of his message to us today, but contrary to the
impression my last few paragraphs may have given it is not all doom
and gloom.

I feel we live in amazing times and are undergoing as great a shift in
collective consciousness as the retreat of the last ice age was for our
ancestors. For me his message is one of optimism, belief, and giving
or hope, faith and charity take your pick. We do have the technology
and we all still have our primitive drive to survive. Our only
choice seems to be that of collective survival harmonising with individual
needs.

There are many 'eco projects' in operation all over the globe that are
through active intervention and education attempting to both manifest
positive physical change and inform the next generation of conservators.
One such example here in Britain is the Eden Project in St. Austell,
Cornwall. This once disused quarry has been magically and creatively
transformed into one of the most incredible sights of our times. Three
huge bio-domes housing a massive array of plant life command centre
stage, with wonderful imaginative outdoor gardens and sculptures
surrounding. The aim of the project is one of botanical and ecological
education delivering a positive message of hope and love. The obvious

blending of man and plant through the use of art and design displays the relationship between our species brilliantly. Information is delivered in an imaginative and inspirational way making one feel in awe of nature's generosity and continued bounty. Rather than concentrating on the damage we are inflicting upon the Earth and its Green Life the centre seems to be saying,

> *'Look, look at how beautiful I am, see my many faces and guises, long to taste my fruits, listen to my branches in the wind, breath in my exotic perfumes, reach out gently to feel my heart, and sense my spirit within'.*

This project is ongoing and will evolve each season as the people and plants learn more and more about one another. I highly recommend you visit it if at all possible and give them your support for the great work they are doing in bringing man and nature closer together again.

In this country alone we have many public and private gardens large and small open to view throughout part and in some cases all of the year. These places can really inspire us and although they are in no part natural they still reflect nature and man working in conjunction as a team. Some may argue the Green Man's natural environment is simply the few remaining wild woodlands but I disagree. True, natural ancient woodland is where his energy is at its most potent, but one can feel his presence elsewhere.

Once connected to nature's spirit people invariably feel a need to simplify their lives by reducing their levels of consumption and increasing their desire to lead a more spiritually fulfilling life. Money is still an issue, as are resources required to survive, but the emphasis seems to shift towards creativity, and love, inspired by nature in all its glorious seasons and diversity. I am constantly meeting people who are 'waking up' as it were to the unhappiness they have created for themselves in their self-propelled lives of acquisition of wealth. Although many of them have all the financial security they could ever need they still feel something is missing but often don't know what.

Once the connection has been made a great transformation often takes place in which their previous desires seem insignificant and futile compared with the immense love and euphoria nature's beauty can offer, free of charge! One such couple I know used to think taking a holiday ensconced in a five star hotel with all its luxury and pampering was the ultimate they could aspire to and for many years this filled their needs. Since connecting with nature on a deeper level they now realise they were missing out and their holidays now range from back

133

packing in Mexico to a week's relaxation at a spiritual retreat. For years they restricted themselves, unaware of what they were missing out on, and its great to hear them excited about the animals and plants they have encountered on these travels rather than having to sit through the endless sameness of their previous holiday recordings.

We all need to re-adjust our priorities and as we do so our demands on nature can be more empathic and less destructive. Like most of humanity I am far from any perception of possible perfection. I am probably much like you, an average person trying to understand better my relationship with my fellow man and my environment. I have faults, addictions and weaknesses built up over forty odd years of living in the western world, but I do my bit when and where I can. My utopia would be to live on the edge of a small almost self-sufficient community devoid of rules and regulations where everyone got a fair share of the cake and all were treated equally, but I am not stupid and know that in reality this doesn't happen.

I am not a communist; instead I prefer to think of myself as a harmonist.

I believe as do many others that we can re-learn the importance of eco-balance from the experiences and knowledge of our pre-industrial past. By taking the best of the past and integrating it with the best of the now we could be on the verge of harmonising.

Many people are choosing a more holistic approach towards life these days and for those already indulging the benefits are obvious. Some of these methods contain many of the old tried and tested herbal remedies that in the most part offer us a more natural way of healing. It is a great worry and concern to those that do practise herb craft that the policies regarding their usage are, ironically, under attack from government bodies who allegedly distrust them, and drug companies keen to continue making their quick buck. Their current viewpoint appears to be that they are untested and therefore unreliable. For many people this is laughable, as one would like to believe that thousands of years of application should be enough proof of their positive benefits and potential side effects. Also, ironically, many of our modern drugs are let loose into circulation without stringent testing due to them being hybrids of existing drugs already tested. There are naturally some dangerous and debatable practices that we should avoid and to exemplify this I will tell you an all too familiar story I have heard on my travels. A woman came to see me for a reading and it transpired she had become involved with a local cult. Under their influence she was taught to believe that every negative thing that ever happened to her was directly her fault and that she could heal her cervical cancer cells without surgery.

In theory this is possible but it relies upon total unequivocal belief, something few of us have. This lady's belief was strong but she had an element of doubt nagging away in her subconscious, which she had become aware of. I felt her reading verified this doubt and also showed that she was in a position of potential danger. Deep down she admitted she knew this too and planned to do something about it, conventionally. My own personal view is that to be holistic in today's society means being able to use all methods at our disposal, surgery included. Thankfully she has seen sense and is now using both western and eastern healing methods. The Chinese, for example, always offer people the choice of eastern or western medicine, or both combined, and this is probably the best way forward for the majority. Medicine is just one example of how we can mix and blend the old ways with the new in our society. Tree medicine is powerful stuff and can have almost miraculous effects at times but our own belief must be strong in order for it to work such magic. The same can be said of the many and varied healing energies people are now working with. For some, whose faith is absolute self-healing, is a possibility but one should not carry any guilt for visiting a doctor. There are a great many charlatans making lots of money out of healing, let's not forget that.

It's always easy to talk the talk but what about walking the walk?

There are tendencies amongst some of the self-proclaimed intellec-tually biased community to lean far too heavily upon that which they learn by reading. Now this is indeed a book and you are reading it but I would like to believe that you get out into the Green Man's true envir-onment occasionally. This concerns me a little and maybe in saying this I am guilty of judgement, but that is not my wish. I am drawn to natural-ists, people from all walks of life who choose to spend their lives involved whether working full time or voluntarily, with nature and in particular trees. Some of these people may not consider themselves spiritual but in many cases their love and respect for our natural environment is obvious and hugely fulfilling for them. They are most definitely feeding their souls by contacting with nature's spirit whether they choose to acknowledge this or not. For those of us claiming spiritual awareness, whatever our beliefs or paths, contact with nature's spirit should be even more enriching.

There are many people living in today's society who could benefit from regular contact with our friend the Green Man. Those who suffer from depression may find it beneficial for although modern drugs and plants such as St. John's Wort have their uses as a natural anti-depressant I am completely convinced that regular exposure to our native woodland would help such folk. Light, fresh air and the natural beauty of our environment can lift fallen spirits better than any artificial man-made drug, that's for sure. When we cut ourselves off from our natural cycles and rhythms we become morose and negative (shift workers suffer from this); we need to get back in touch with our inner drum and listen to its beat. By doing this we can alleviate many of the side effects of modern life. I am not suggesting that this will work for everyone, as some reasons for depression are very serious and need extensive psychiatric treatment, but for the average workaday blues it works well.

In our attempts to make life easier we have detached ourselves from the natural world, not entirely but partially, and even though this partial detachment has its benefits it also leaves something 'wanting'. In this hi-tech digital age we are constantly under bombardment by communicative energy whether we are sensitive to this or not, and it concerns many of us that these digital pulses may not be that good for us. There is already enough evidence relating to mobile phones that gives us all cause for concern.

It is probably almost impossible to escape this invisible intruder into our lives but the positive benefits currently outweigh the potential side effects. Yes, I own a mobile. I gave in grudgingly a year ago and must admit it has added a positive aspect to my life but as with every new gadget I worry about the downside. My generation is possibly the last in the western world that remembers life without videos, calculators, computers, microchips, mobile phones etc. but for my daughter's generation this is the norm as much as television and cars were for us but not our parents. Like many of my peer group I love this new technology and without it writing would definitely be problematic for me as I have lost full use of my dominant hand after an accident.

So how do I as an initiate of the Green Man balance this dichotomy? By believing that it can be done responsibly and without the need for complete rape and pillage of our natural environment. I also believe that it is part of our mutual evolution to travel this road if only to find ourselves back where we started. One example is that we have more than enough plastic in current circulation to keep us all happy for many years to come. The only problem is the cost of re-cycling such products. Maybe I am an ignorant fool in trusting my fellow man but as we are all fifty percent vegetable I can't see the present imbalance lasting too much longer.

If we as a race wish to maintain our present life styles some unavoidable compromises will have to be made and I am sure they will be in the not too distant future.

But are these compromises negative? No, not all of them. It would be far better for us to be putting our agricultural efforts into increasing organic farming rather than genetic engineering. Organic farming works in harmony with its environment, using natural predators as pesticides and coupled with high technology it could work very well if only governments ploughed more funds into it. But big seed and chemical companies subsidise politics so until that situation changes we will have to force the change ourselves by altering our eating and spending. That's all very well, I hear you cry, but what if you cannot afford organic food? True, it is more expensive and as yet lacks the out-of-season choices we have all become used to. So as a moderate harmoniser and rather than preach what I don't as yet practise wholeheartedly why not just start including it when you can. For those of you with green fingers and an aptitude for gardening why not grow some of your own fruit and veg – if you have time that is. Even if we all started buying fifty percent organic we would make a huge impact on demand so increasing production and government funding, see? I know of people living on state benefits who do it, so it can't be that difficult. The benefits globally and individually far outweigh the reticence towards a slightly increased food bill. Simply by gradually introducing more organic food into your diet you will feel the positive benefits. If, for example, you are a meat eater, wouldn't you rather eat a happy pig than an unhappy one? It really does taste better, honestly, go on try it. It may be the price we all have to pay but in the long run it will be appreciated by future generations. Of course in the mean time our cutting-edge science may well come up with nano-technology capable of creating everything we need without taking any more from Gaia's diminishing stocks and allow the planet to breathe a sigh of immense relief. That is if the super-bugs don't get us first.

What on earth has all this got to do with making a connection and his message?

His message is simple. Here is one such example:

I am you and you are me
This is all that we will be
But love will out from every tree
Our dance goes on eternally

That is one such direct contact.

137

He means: We are both made of the same stuff although we are biological and he botanical; these are our interpretations and scientific labels we have given ourselves.

We are born, we live, we reproduce and eventually we die just like trees. Our bodies contain many life forms that depend on our existence for their survival, just like trees.

Trees breathe out oxygen and as such have roots that helped created biological oxygen-breathing creatures like us exist in the first place. We are completely co-dependent. We cannot live without each other. Trees give love unconditionally as we can do too if we allow ourselves to. The dance relates to our active conscious relationship and respect. The eternal living dance.

Just by taking an ethical and moral first step in his direction you will be adding to the increasing numbers of people today who are doing the same thing. Whilst we continue to buy into this unnatural world we have created we will be condoning the actions of genetic farming and its inevitable knock-on effect on our eco-system. I am not an expert or radical activist and my knowledge is limited but I am prepared to pay the extra cost as it has immediate benefits which in turn will affect my offspring in the future. I currently live in the heart of England's market garden where much of the testing for genetic crops is taking place. Judging by the tiny organic sections in local supermarkets I presume local demand is not high for healthy food. Saturated fats, sugar and alcohol seem to have pride of place on our supermarket shelves sadly. My brothers, on the other hand, live in the East End of London where organic food is fast increasing in popularity amongst enlightened consumers. Considering the area I live in has a long history of intensive agriculture and London's residents by and large command larger salaries this is not that surprising.

But food is only part of his message. Every interaction between people and nature has an effect on the eco-system and always has. He is laughing at me as I write this as he knows the truth and through him we can learn it too. Our interaction may well have some effect but the spirit of nature is collectively far more powerful than us regardless of the obvious damage we inflict upon it. Nature itself invented purging and general arse kicking, a fact we could all do well to remember just in case we are ever tempted to become complacent. His message is 'love me and I'll love you' in some respects but this isn't the simple human emotion we relate it to. The love of the Green Man is eternal, everlasting, and infinitely durable for as long as he continues to reign. This love is pulling us tugging us, evoking inside us, calling us back to face him and appreciate his cycle. For it is our own. Like a perfect lover he stimulates all our senses through smell, sight, hearing, taste and touch and as such a perfect being he loves us with all his spirit. He is all-forgiving, all-seeing, all-knowing, all-caring and wants us to give in return. But what must we give? Do we all have to become idealists with the highest green ethics and morals? No, surprisingly not. Obviously it is up to each and every one of us to wrestle with our own conscience over the issue but ultimately he wants what any lover wants and that is attention and appreciation. He knows only too well that the only way we can collectively avert our own demise is by simply loving him more.

How on Earth can this simple act change anything? Easily if you think about it. Just imagine how much better our environment would become if just a five percent increase in appreciation of nature occurred within our collective souls each year. As soon as the loving relationship begins it has a transforming affect on those who have attained it. Many of you reading this book may already be practising such a relationship and be way ahead of your global community. This is good. You are the guides, for it is through your practice and work that others can hear his message. But whilst the majority of this planet is run the way it is we have to find ways of communicating this message to all and for that reason his words have to resonate with the widest audience possible.

Oh Hawthorn tree Oh Hawthorn tree
You give your love so generously
Spare a branch for me to see
A new love soon Oh Hawthorn tree

(Example of common love spell carried out when you see the first hawthorn blossom)

As I travel around my local environment I am touched by the inordinate love and respect most people have put into their gardens. It is obvious to me that deep down we all have an ingrained desire for nature's beauty. As a nation we are great gardeners, creating little mini eco-systems for a diverse selection of creatures and plants to live in. I don't think it will have escaped your notice that the explosion of home improvement programmes and garden makeover shows are influencing how many people now view their environment. For many of us the repetitive sameness of these productions can get tedious but they have their uses and are certainly encouraging people to specifically appreciate that which is beautiful over that which is most definitely not. I'm not saying that they always get it right and some of the creations are designed purely around the aesthetics rather than any long-term ecological benefit.

Ideally many of us want our own little piece of Eden and I feel this is a step in the right direction, but it would be better if some of the garden designers left the concrete out. Inwardly our spirit knows what it wants and for all of us this is a shared human need.

We all need fresh air, fresh water, safe and healthy food, clothing, shelter, healing and love. Everything else is above basic survival and one could argue superfluous.

Many of you reading this book are probably environmentally aware souls already living a more ecological lifestyle and if so I apologise for re-emphasising these issues but they are relevant none the less.

The world we now live in has become infinitely complicated and has evolved through our imaginations applied in an attempt to simplify our acquisition of these basic requirements for life. We are unique in the way we visualise our world on this inner level and are obviously brilliant at manifesting that which we so desire. Unfortunately it is only over the past fifty years or so that our impact has gone beyond that which Gaia can sustain at this present rate of consumption. One could argue that it is merely a reflection of Darwin's theory of survival of the fittest that has placed us on the brink of this current potential disaster and if so it won't be us in the west that survive. It will be the people who really are fitter. Ironically although much of the so-called developing world's populations are periodically underfed they are probably much fitter. They are better placed to resist germs and have far stronger immune systems than us softies in the west. They are better at going without and can survive conditions we would crumble under in just a few weeks. Their needs are still the basic survival requirements, some of which are still not met on a daily basis. When in the Bible it mentions the meek inheriting the Earth I tend to think of those people.

Eradicating third-world debt and redistributing resources is a step in the right direction and it seems politically this attitude is beginning to shift. But to enable those who have nothing to begin fending for themselves we must be prepared to have less. And therein lies the problem. The Green Man wants his green world back. He is fed up with our pollution, our greed, and fearful of our nuclear capabilities. How do I know this? We all know this. England truly is a green and pleasant land, by and large, but we are far from perfect and our agricultural and industrial scars still litter the landscape. Even those of us that allow our gardens to become scenes of re-forestation are benefiting the environment by neglect, as undisturbed clean gardens will attract creatures needing privacy. Waste seems to be one of our greatest problems, with chemical toxins, plastics and radioactive substances being the worst offenders. We will all have to pay for this and perhaps our drastically increasing local tax bills reflect this. I can see a time coming soon where we will be fined or penalised for excess waste, which may well be the only way to increase awareness for some. As a potential consequence people may well choose to buy products with less packaging and in so doing start thinking about their own personal effect upon the environment. It does seem unfair though, as to implement this radical step will still leave the rich able to afford such spoils. To implement this last minute pull back from the brink we all require drastic changes. These are about to be forced upon us from our government agencies and will occur globally and locally. We are about to pay for the damage the literal sins of the fathers have created as I write. Over the past fifty years or so we have been given options and choices that have far exceeded our needs and now we will be forced to slim down. There are no simple solutions and the onus will still be on each and every one of us but we need to start changing our habits before we are forced to, as this will not only help lessen the radical responses we can expect but also strengthen us for the future. I feel our emphasis should be a spiritual one regardless of specific path but this might only be a romantic dream. Some share this dream and it is with love and compassion for humanity as a whole that many of the leaders of these indoctrinated paths are questioning some of the validity of their dogma in today's society and moving towards encouraging their 'flocks' to be far more accepting of each other. This is a brave step forward and one that modern pagans both helped initiate and are beginning to play a larger part in. This is all good. I'm not in favour of a New World Order controlled by a pre-dominantly Western global economy within the current world situation. Too many other issues need dealing with first such as debt, starvation, health, and a reduction in individual consumption before any global solutions can be found to problems such as terrorism and war.

But let's allow ourselves to dream of interfaith tolerance, re-distribution of land and wealth, free social services, obligatory re-cycling, backed up with minimum impact sustainability is possible without the loss of identity, culture and language.

We are going to be forced into a massive change in circumstances, whether we like it or not, and ironically we in the west will feel the hardships worst. As the fuel runs out (predicted within ten to thirty years' time) many of us will be forced into leaving our cars at home unless of course we are all running around in hydrogen fuelled vehicles by then which, again, I doubt. The emphasis of priority where fuel is concerned will be on haulage companies responsible for the transportation of food and emergency supplies. In this country it is possible that many of our redundant waterways could be reinstated for movement of luxury goods and possibly our railways will be expanded, but again this is all speculation. The use of natural Gaia energy will become more prolific as we begin to see the increase in use of wind and solar power. This will be a much welcomed change for the better. There will be a global reduction in production of useless plastic waste and a certain plastic doll we all know may well have had her day. Shame. As the old industrial age has passed and we adjust to this new technological age of micro every-thing a new age of preservation will possibly emerge where the throw-away products of the past fifty years are gradually replaced by sustainable products that are infinitely repairable and durable. Imagine owning a washing machine that lasts for life, and I mean life! How will we pay for such longevity? Where is the buck to be made out of eternal products? Where is the money going to come from? We are entering the age of eternal credit and this Orwellian vision could have its positive upside. If people were to enter the totally cashless society without resorting to intrusive microchips or laser tattoos there might be a way for sustainable economics combined with capitalist principles. These ideals would alter, as spiritually inspired market forces demanded low impact goods and chattels. Much higher prices would be placed upon luxury items and would reflect more accurately their cost to the planet. All these ideas and many others are constantly being updated and evol-ving in Green politics. The Green Parties across the globe are trying to face this humungous mountain we all have to climb with a positive outlook. Instead of painting a bleak future they are bravely going forth exploring new horizons and attempting to implement new civilizations in a future of harmonious growth eternally re-cycled. We have two choices as far as I can see: we either get rid of money, which I feel is unlikely in the extreme, or we turn our attention to new industries. What new industries? Clean-up industries for one, responsible for safely dismantling the old defunct ones and replacing them with new eco-friendly businesses. What kind of eco-friendly businesses? Good question. I think we will still have more or less the same ones but they will have to be harmless to the environment or heavily penalised financially if not. I don't see why we as individuals should have to start paying extra. If the business world were offered an initial financial incentive to implement these changes they would. Basically as we all know anything that generates money is attractive to business and anything that costs is not. Penalising businesses will therefore work.

8

These changes will have to occur and in reality we all know this and for those whose love and respect for nature is strongest the changes will be relatively easy. For those who currently have nothing the effects will be beneficial. But for the rest . . .

Two friends are out shopping and one says to the other, 'I like that dress'
She wants to possess it
The other looks and says, 'Uh huh'.
The first girl buys the dress. 'I'm so glad I have this dress', she says.
She possesses it.
The second girl says, 'Uh huh'.
The first girl wants more response from her friend and is desirous of promoting envy in her. 'Are you with us, hello is anyone at home?' she says to provoke her friend.
'Oh sorry, I was watching that little boy with his friend sharing an ice cream. Look at their faces covered in strawberry. They do look funny'.
The first girl is upset, 'So you'd rather watch kids eating ice cream than look at my new dress. Great'.

What does this tell us?
The first girl wants to own the dress so she buys it, thus achieving her desire, but the desire is also to make her friend jealous. The dress will give her a brief and transient pleasure. The manipulation of her friend was wasted energy.
She enjoyed a brief and transient pleasure.
The friend enjoyed watching the children so much she was oblivious to her friend's intentions.
She will always find pleasure.
Another story with almost exactly the same relevance occurred a few years ago in spring. I invited a small group of friends to join me on a loosely guided walk through some ancient coppiced woodland. Many of them spent most of the walk staring closely at the ground in front of their feet and a few studied the fauna and flora whilst looking up their observations in books. The odd one or two did actually attempt to just 'connect' and I feel that for them something beautiful happened. As we bimbled slowly through the carpets of wild garlic one of them decided he had to possess a small clump of it in spite of my protests against this course of action and explanation as to why I objected. Happy with his apparent possession we walked on.
By the time we returned to the car park his bunch of once happy jubilant garlic had reduced itself to a limp withered sacrifice. My only

comment at the time was, if I remember correctly, something along the lines of, 'I hope it was worth it for you'.

He had a brief and transient attempt at possessing nature whilst nature responded by dying in his hands. I haven't seen him again.

Do you look at nature and think, if only I could buy the ocean?
I want to own that tree?
That cloud is mine?
No!
Nature is yours forever but you cannot possess it.

The land may be occupied by your family but they cannot take it when they die nor can their children.

We are the caretakers of Earth and as the most successful, intelligent and most destructive life form upon it we have, in part, become responsible for it. For the damage at least.

The Earth has given us life; now it is time for us to surrender to her before she is forced to respond to our impact and threaten our very existence. We are threatening her, and in turn her link to us, the Green Man.

But something wonderful is happening and in terms of evolution this is a giant leap in collective awareness. We are connecting with Gaia on a conscious level and as such many people are becoming aware of this energy and all it has to offer.

More and more of us in the western developed world are experiencing the void of uselessness that our consumer based society offers and turning back to the spirit of nature to give us deeper meaning in life. No longer happy with the quick fix of a day of retail therapy we are searching for a longer fix, if you like. Work and the endless quest for wealth has become tedious and stressful, leaving many people cash-rich but time-poor. The one thing most working parents want most is free time coupled with enough to keep them within the 'comfort zone' they have created. Often it is this zone that causes the problems in the first place. By re-prioritising in a more spiritual direction we can simplify our zone and still have creature comforts, just adjusted ones. Spirit calls from nature as it is nature and wants us to enjoy her bounty. By eating quality food more frequently, getting outside more often, being loving and giving on a more regular basis on all levels from intimate sacred sex to global love we begin to step away from the constraints of modern life.

Even those resigned to life amongst the concrete towers of city dwellings struggling each day through the milling crowds can stop occasionally and take some real notice of the nature they have on their doorstep. They can create little oasis of their own to communicate with, whether it be a humble window box or a plot taken on in a nearby allotment (most areas have them even in inner cities) and extend this relationship further. They can look up at the skies and take note of the birds that fly about and watch the fairy seeds floating in the air. They can watch the moon go through its cycle and feel the emotional link we all have with her. They can actually go outside (OK, I know some people are unfortunately housebound) and walk until they find a quiet spot to sit and just be. Most of our larger cities in this country have plenty of nature to look at. It's simply a matter of seeing the wood for the trees. Failing all the above you can get a rail card and escape the throngs to the countryside for the day. Even the London Underground connects with suburban and country areas that are accessible without too much cost involved. There are very few excuses for the majority of us and only the very few are truly trapped or dependent on others for their mobility.

If you are unfortunately housebound try praying or 'calling' for help and trust it will be answered. Call out from your heart to the universe and if your desire is strong enough someone will hear your call and respond'. Believe and it will be.

Everything we are and everything we have been creates our future, so to claim ignorance these days is futile. We have judged ourselves and found ourselves wanting if we didn't we wouldn't have conscience. Conscience is awareness of fault and knowledge of wrong and right but in nature there are no wrongs or rights, only nature.

Nature accepts her faults and sees them as necessary or else they wouldn't occur. We are products of nature's faults – mutants you could say. Evolutionary leaps occur when nature appears to cock up but the mutation or original fault creates a new dimension of being and allows new opportunities. Think of speech, for example. Once nature altered one person's vocal chords this mutation allowed for noises to be produced and as we took that to be a positive benefit nature reproduced the fault until everyone could talk. Now think of all the languages old and new that have evolved from this mutation and consider all that has been achieved by speech. What to nature was a fault to us became an advantage and proves that if we all collectively desire something it happens. This is one way of interacting with nature.

But think of the consequences and think long and hard imagine, if you can, a world evolved without speech.

I love silence, silence is truly golden.

145

Human biologists and anthropologists might argue that it was from constantly trying to verbally communicate that we stretched our vocal chords allowing speech but which ever way it happened it was still deviant.

How often can you truly say 'I am happy in silence'? I don't know the answer. That is for you to know but for those who dislike silence I say, why?

Do your thoughts disturb you?

Are you unhappy with your memories?

If so perhaps you need to calm your mind.

Silencing the mind of words is difficult for some but is an essential step towards harmonising with nature and finding your central calm being. At the core of our planet there is a magnetic pole that runs more or less constantly north to south.

We are all connected to this magnetism. It keeps all the particles of Gaia together – it is Gaia's centred self. As reflections of her creative force we too have this calm inner pole. Mystics have long known this, as have all who practise meditation. When you reach that state of inner calm, silence, love and peace your sense of time disappears, as does your outer everyday persona. You just are. Reaching this place connects you with every inner particle of the universe and you realise you are love expressed. You can experience many unusual things on the road to this place. Some people get a buzzing sensation around their third eye, positioned just above and between their eyebrows. Some people get colours either externally or internally visualised. Some people get sensations of being patted gently on the head or spider's web sensations running down their faces. Some people feel extraordinary energy flowing up and down their spines and glowing all around them. Some people feel like they have become detached from their environment and lose sensation of their physical bodies.

For some there is increased psychic ability and telepathy or genuine knowing but in truth we become mirrors reflecting off one another.

A sense of euphoria like a wave flows through them and as it passes it is replaced with inner peace and calm acceptance that all is well and always will be. This experience is unlikely to last for any discernible length of time unless you are an avatar or pure expression of the divine and for most of us that isn't the case. But even to touch briefly upon divinity is divine and for most of us it is sufficient that we can go to this place and find rest and recuperation as and when we need it.

The path has its equal light and dark, however, and for those people carrying large amounts of negative energy it will be a hard task master, for to face divinity means to surrender and let go – something many people are afraid to do.

As she gazed out upon the morning dew she felt nostalgic but it was a warm nostalgia born out of love for the beauty of nature. Her father had died that day and she missed him already. The dew reassured her that some things never change and that it would always be there for her to appreciate. She concerted to remember the good times and surrender to the bad. The sun lit up the dew and magically revealed the delicate lace of spiders' webs covering the grass. His spirit still spoke to her and she could imagine his artist's eye appreciating their joint vista of natures beauty. As the sun disappeared so did the web but she had that moment before she let him go.

Being in constant touch with nature's cycles helps us understand many of the more intense feelings we occasionally have and to realise their place in our lives. Intensity has its place but to dwell on any emotion is potentially harmful. We cannot simply allow ourselves to be emotional slaves. It is denying our intellect to do so. We cannot arrogantly think we transcend nature either, for even conscious awareness is part of nature's creation. But we can attempt to balance ourselves and learn how to heal our own inner ills. All these things are possible and for every one person that does it several will be positively energised by the experience. If you heal yourself you are helping to heal the world. All of us need healing from time to time and I don't just mean a trip to the chemist for some painkillers. We need inner spiritual cleansing.

Connecting with our ancient places transforms us on this inner plane just as meditation can, but to combine both is as close as any of us will get to God/divine force etc. Nature holds a key to this inner mystery and yet it is so easy to connect with that for many people it is a case of not being able to see the proverbial wood for the trees.

Many people I talk to say,

'Do you want to take us back to the Stone Age?'

No, beyond it if possible, is my answer.

Intellectually we are as much in the Stone Age today as our ancestors were but would you consider it wise to arm a chimpanzee with a loaded gun?

Others say,

147

'Are you not scared for the future?'

No, I accept that what will be will be and is obviously meant to be or else it wouldn't be.

Trees do this every day. They are all competing amongst themselves for resources and the right to light. They have parameters to live within and live to the best of each of their abilities. But I do think there is tree karma though, or at least it appears so. Some trees don't survive much past conception, just like us, some make it to childhood but no further, just like us, some get so far and are then beaten by bigger stronger trees in the race for nutrients and light. We do too and yet many reach maturity and some go on for a considerable time very much as we do. So it appears in nature there is a time for everyone and everyone has their time. But if eternity is in one second then we all exist eternally. Once we be, we be, basically.

A friend I walked with one day asked me, 'Do you hug trees then?'

I laughed because I had indeed tried hugging trees but due to my preference for oak I'd found that not many of them are very easy or comfortable to hug. Try bear hugging an ancient oak for example: they are a bit hard and lumpy. Little trees are probably easier to hug should you wish to.

My answer was 'No, but I like to lean against them, sit under them and when younger and more agile I enjoyed climbing them'. There are many ways to hug trees.

His message is bursting forth with new vigour every spring and as I write during May it is evident all around me. Nature goes bonkers at this time of year and fresh green spring leaves hang heavily from every bough. The grass now needs weekly cutting and the weeds are taking on a new life of their own that far outreaches my attempts at restraint. The early bulbs have passed and carpets of herbivorous borders are blossoming on cue. The birds have given birth and the air is full of their hectic rhythms and skies full of parents hunting for food. Showers replace sunshine and blue sky that in turn replaces showers. The evening light creates a magical presence and warmth that glows inside every living thing. There's a buzz in the air and it has little to do with bees. As the energy increases, teachers have problems controlling over-stimulated youngsters who are being called by their souls to go outside. This is the Green Man. He cares little for exams or our enforced educational system. He wants to share his energy and beauty. He wants us with him at this time of year to play and dance. I have often thought the academic year is geared out of sync with nature and this is probably the worst time of year for study. I myself am finding it increasingly difficult to remain still or focused indoors at the moment and will soon head for the tracks with my dog. He can't understand why we haven't done so already. Rain means little to him.

I often hear, 'I am a white witch' or 'I work with light energies only. How can you work with the dark?'

It is so simple: out of the darkness comes the light. Without the dark there would be no light. When I deliberately focus upon dark I am searching for light. New light.

For three years I worked as an ambulance technician in the London Ambulance Service. It taught me a lot about humanity, especially the eternal cycle of dark and light. I had to face death on a daily basis but I didn't fear it. At first it intrigued me and then I just accepted it regardless of the circumstances. I faced my own mortality and acknowledged its inevitability with no particular emotion attached to it. I discovered that the majority of people die a natural and fairly peaceful death. Only the few die young in our culture and even fewer die in tragic or dreadful circumstances. I surmised that much of the suffering we go through in life could be avoided though.

But whenever I needed a pick-me-up or general spiritual lift I turned my attention to nature and even in such a large metropolis as London there is plenty of nature to look at. I can still remember individual trees planted outside certain hospitals that gave me pleasure whilst I idled away a few minutes after finishing a job. Even if there are no trees in sight nature is never very far away and plants find all kinds of places to make homes. Then there is always the sky and bird life. As I meditated, albeit briefly and inconspicuously, I felt the energy within me rise and I was ready for another call, in theory, but going back to station for a rest was also welcomed.

We have choices but sometimes it is difficult to see clearly as we have veiled the truth from our eyes.

A friend of mine rang up one day with her head full of problems of a romantic nature. She wanted to go for a walk. I agreed thinking that this would indeed clear some of her present confusion. She brought her teenage son along with us and we proceeded to a local park. As we walked along I remained silent whilst she spouted forth like a fountain on full blast, constantly recirculating the same emotion. Her son remained silent also. Whilst he and I admired the landscape of tall beech trees and mature red cedar she kept her head down and talked. Eventually he broke the silence by remarking on a particular tree and I encouraged him to approach it and study it in more detail. He was amazed at its soft spongy bark and network of spider webs that covered this great living being. A deep and profound connection was made and I could feel his loving energy go out with admiration and respect of this new friend. It was at this point that my friend stopped talking and looked around her, and like sleeping beauty waking up after her hundred year sleep she remarked, 'Oh Mary, it's so beautiful here. It's so romantic. Look at that lovely pond and that view'. As she did this her worry lines melted away and her troubled brow lifted, her eyes opened in wonder, and she positively glowed radiantly. The boyfriend returned to the conversation about twenty minutes later but she kept her eyes up and sounded clearer and more positive so I guess the magic worked and she was healed of that particular negative cycle.

When I walk with people I let them be and trust in the Green Man to show them whatever it is they are meant to see. It rarely fails.

I have no idea how long it will take me to write this book or whether I will even scratch the surface of his message today but whenever I need inspiration or guidance I go to source. Even just spending some quality time pottering about in my garden strengthens the link and my head is soon spinning with his visions again.

As I finish writing this chapter I am amazed at a news story just breaking of the Galileo spacecraft being sent into Jupiter's atmosphere for fear it may contaminate possible life on Jupiter's moons. What regard for such hostile environment and one we will never intimately know and yet would that such regard and respect were shown to life here on Earth.

Comical really.

All around the sky is red
Nowhere left to lay my head
Silent heat now escaped
Evidence of nature raped

Darkness falls

The moon shines down
No longer Gaia's holy crown
Tree's are but her memory
There's no one left to hear or see

Or

Vibrant in the green of spring
Now we are truly listening
A landscape of organic fields
Giving us their heavy yields

Gardens bloom vigorously
Helped by hands as industry
The birds sing the water flows
We visit all our wishing wells

The choice is ours.

AUTHOR'S TIPS FOR HARMONISING

- Befriend your local woodlands, parks and forests.
- Buy organic/locally grown produce when you can.
- Re-cycle as much as possible.
- Choose sustainable products when possible.
- Repair rather than replace items if possible.
- Barter with others for goods and services.
- Find an eco-friendly outlet for your creativity.
- Listen to the children they have much to teach us.
- Laugh more.

6

Spiritual Trees

Therefore, with resolution as his only support and companion, he
set his mind on enlightenment and proceeded to the root of a Pipal
Tree (Bo Tree), where the ground was carpeted with green grass.
['Life of Buddha' (as edited by Avril de Silva-Vigier)]

And, yes, he received enlightenment!

We all know how important to us trees are from a resource point of view and as oxygen producers, but what about their spiritual properties?

We will look at that in a moment, but first a little glance back at the changes in the lives of our trees. Trees are some of the oldest beings on this planet.

Our English oak, for example, can live for over one thousand years. It is hard sometimes to imagine that our country was once largely covered in mature forests. It's easy to forget that our landscape has undergone a dramatic change since agriculture really took off. Trying to imagine how it must have been even a few hundred years ago is difficult for us. Sadly we have become used to our cities, towns, roads and industry but we also have to face the inordinate damage we have inflicted upon the Earth. We know how and why this situation changed. Starting with clearing for agriculture, then Church and house building, tree desecration really took off with the shipbuilding industry in medieval times. This then continued for many hundreds of years.

Now we have very few ancient woodlands left. Luckily those that have remained are heavily protected on the whole, mainly by conservation organisations.

If you really want to get hands-on experience and learn about woodland many of these organizations regularly need volunteers. We've listed some of these at the back of the book. The work can be very rewarding on all levels. Although we have by and large lost our

155

once great forests we can usually all find mature trees near where we live. Even a wise old lone beech tree in a modern park can offer a magical experience. Nature in general appreciates positive attention. We have all heard of people who talk or play music to their plants and swear it helps them grow. Well, it's the same for all living things. We all react positively to friendly and loving vibrations. You can put this to the test very simply.

Try growing two identical plants; tomatoes for example. Give each of them the same amount of earth, water and light. One of them you must completely ignore, the other one you must be nice to. You'll be amazed at the results.

MAGICAL TREES

All trees have their own magical properties. Starting with birch, let's take a short journey with the most commonly used of the Celtic Tree Ogham.

BIRCH

We've begun with birch for many reasons, one of these being that birch is often the first tree to colonize new areas of potential woodland. Initially, perhaps this is why it has long been thought of as the tree of new beginnings? It is a tree with essentially female qualities. Being an extremely watery tree this connection is not surprising as women have slightly more water in them than men. It is also a very graceful and slender tree that seems to dance in the breeze and has less than you would expect in foliage for a tree of its size. The silver birch seen by moonlight has a beautiful enchanted atmosphere as the light reflects off its bark.

Sunlight also has a magical effect on the tree and brings out all the more subtle colours in the bark.

Like the grass snakes that are often drawn to its moist environment it too sheds its skin from time to time. This bark was used long ago as early writing paper.

The traditional besom (witch's) broom is partly made from birch twigs.

Birch is therefore associated with cleansing and clearing, magically as well as literally.

Being a tree of high water content it is connected elementally with our emotions and therefore feelings of love. Norse tradition links birch with Frigga, the goddess of love, marriage, the clouds and healing. Birch and Beltane, the May fire festival of fertility and love, are joined by the use of birch twigs to light the Beltane fire. There's a lovely Welsh custom that involves the giving of a birch garland by the man to the woman he loves hoping she will return one to him as a confirmation of her feelings being the same. This supposes they both know of the custom of course.

Birch sap can be collected quite easily by boring a small (about one inch) hole in the trunk and draining it off with a small length of tubing. The sap from birch has many uses.

It should be taken in early spring before the leaves arrive. The bark of the birch has anaesthetic and antiseptic qualities. If taking some bark, as with all things we help ourselves to in nature, we should ask first and not forget to say thank you afterwards. When cutting some bark of any tree it's important not to circle the tree – this will kill it. It is excellent for use in hard water areas where kidney stones can be a problem. The leaves made into a tea will help flush the kidneys and bladder. It's cleansing properties make it ideal as an ingredient for massage oil. It is most beneficial as a cure for acne and scurf. Meditating on birch will give you greater healing abilities, both to use on the pain of others and any you might get.

Magical workings for love, healing and birth of new ideas, including the use of birch, will be greatly empowered. Sweeping your circle with a birch besom will purify and clear your space. Eostre, the Anglo-Saxon goddess of spring, was often invoked around birch trees. Birch is often referred to as the 'Lady of the woods'.

ROWAN

This unassuming tree is a bit of a loner. It prefers the company of other species rather than growing among clumps of its own kind. It only usually reaches a maximum height of around thirty feet and was frequently planted in coppiced woodland to offer protection to saplings. The rowan's red berries are a particular delicacy for birds that are often found singing in a state of gastronomic bliss close by in late summer and early autumn. The bark is shiny and smooth, of a rusty colour, and has horizontal lines on it. The leaves are curled in spring and fairly slim like ash. Unlike ash the leaves are set alternately. It blooms in May with clumps of tiny white flowers.

Rowan has many links to the old gods and goddesses. In Ireland it is Brigid's tree and Brigantia here in England. The tree's wood was highly prized for the making of spinning wheels, which tied in with some of the qualities associated with these two goddesses. In ancient Greece its very conception is a result of squabbling between Zeus and his daughter Hebe. He entrusted a magical cup into her care, which she managed to lose to some demons. Zeus was enraged at his daughter's irresponsibility and an eagle was sent to retrieve the cup from the demons. During the resulting struggle every time a drop of eagle's blood fell to earth there a rowan tree grew.

Magically it has the power to rejuvenate. This obviously meant it was held in great esteem in ancient times. **Warning:** Rowan berries are generally considered poisonous, especially to children.

The rowan provides astringent and antibiotic medicine. Meditating with the tree lifts the spirits and encourages a sense of calm. It offers protection against any unwanted magic from others. The red berries of the rowan signalled a danger to any evil spirits and was planted anywhere that protection was required. Thus they were often found planted to mark sacred places or ley lines. Seasonally you can use rowan on Imbolc which is traditionally Brigid's day and heralds the spring with its tiny buds.

Beltane gave rowan an opportunity to prove its protective worth by the placing of it over milk sheds to ward off any evil influences. Carrying it on midsummer's night will protect people from being affected by faerie folk. Tables at harvest time (Lammas) were decorated with rowan berries.

For a little tree there's a lot to be said for it.

ALDER

Alder is another water loving tree. It is frequently found growing amongst birch, willow and hazel. You will often find it with willows alongside streams and brooks. The place I grew up in is called Aldersbrook for obvious reasons. It's not one of the biggest of our native trees, usually only reaching up to seventy feet in height. It is a broadleaf tree and the only one to produce small almost pinecone-like catkins. Its bark is brown to black and furrowed in almost straight lines. When cut the bark will reveal a pinkish red underneath and appears to bleed. This led to many a superstition in the past. It was thought by some to harbour an evil spirit and was treated with the greatest respect as a consequence. Old German legends link it with elves and it is known as the elf king.

The Celts had a healthy regard for this tree and would use it for charcoal making specifically if the charcoal was later to be used in furnaces for making weapons. The red sap would also be used as a dye for faces before battle. Seasonally it has associations with March, often a lean month in the past. This was a time when winter provisions would run out and people would go hungry.

Elementally it is unique in having all four represented in it. Air as a result of its whistle-making tradition – its roots are nourished by the Earth, Fire is bound up with Irish tradition, stating that to cut down an alder will cause your house to burn in return and Water by its own preference for it.

As a healer Alder offers help emotionally, by helping us to come to terms with them and be more objective. Inflammation can be reduced with its bark by making it into a cold poultice and applying it to the area. The leaves have the same qualities and can be used freshly, applied where there is swelling and pain. It is definitely the tree of the bi-sexual, having both female and male qualities. It encourages us to try for balance in our lives and is very useful in elemental magic and all solitary workings. If you need protection when dealing with unavoidable confrontations carry a piece of alder with you.

WILLOW

Willows are fairly commonplace in this country but despite this fact, they are rarely anything less than dramatic in their landscape. Willows, like alder, are fond of riverbanks. Their branches often grow down, sweeping romantically into the water below. They stay with the flow and encourage us to allow our emotions to flow through us enabling understanding, growth and healing to take place. The willow as a meditative aid is great for clearing unwanted emotional blockages.

The tree itself is unmistakable with its thin wispy branches and narrow leaves. Many were pollarded in the past and still show signs of it today. The branches were extremely useful for basket making amongst other things, and still are. Most willows have long tapered leaves that are usually silver underneath. They produce catkins as fruit and when ripe the seeds appear as little wispy down in the wind.

Being another watery tree, it is associated primarily with goddess energy. It is also a tree of the underworld. Willows are linked with the crone and dark goddess phases of the moon. The very old superstition of knocking on wood originates from willow and it is considered very unlucky to burn it.

For healing purposes willow has to be most famous for its aspirin-like qualities. The bark contains salicylic acid. This made it an excellent pain reliever for conditions such as rheumatism and arthritis.

It is considered a tree of immortal status due to its almost unique abilities to never entirely die. Even when a large old tree finally collapses and gives all the appearance of being dead up will sprout new growth and the cycle starts all over again. This explains its underworld connections. Willow therefore can gain us insight into the past and also our futures.

It is a very useful wood to have around when grieving for it helps us to understand our grief better and come to terms with it by putting it into perspective.

It is a great tree to use as a meditive aid for prophetic reasons, and for poetic and literal inspiration too. A balm made of willow bark, its leaves and its seed will help with improving your psychic abilities when massaged into the third eye (between eyebrows) before meditation. This balm will also be useful as a topical application to infections of the throat or strained vocal chords. Willow is the ideal tree to use for any rituals at Samhain. Due to its eternal quality it can help you to connect with the spirits of the dead. Should you wish to, of course.

Tying a knot in a thin shoot of willow will help to bring love to you.

ASH

The ash tree is commonly known as the World Tree in ancient Norse and druid legend.

All humanity is believed to have originated from this great tree. It grows tall and straight (as a rule) and its roots stretch deeper than those of many of its friends in the forest.

The bark is green/grey and smooth when young, making it very popular to carve. The leaves are narrow and act as a channel for water to run down, allowing the stem to absorb it. Ash loves water. The leaf buds or fruit are like little helicopter blades swirling to the ground in autumn. They don't root until the following year, however.

Ash is a favourite tree for coppicing as its wood has a variety of uses.

It is one of the few woods that will actually burn when green and therefore makes an ideal all year round log source. The handles of besom brooms were and indeed still are primarily made from ash. It is considered mature when it reaches around forty to fifty years old and stands at around 150 feet. Being highly elastic it has always been associated with bow making.

To enter the magical world of the ash is to become a traveller in time for it is believed that the ash is the gateway to the past, present and future.

The roots stretch deep down into the underworld giving us access to the past. The trunk itself represents our present which hopefully is purposeful and strong and the outer branches and leaves are our potential futures.

Meditating by an ash tree will help you reach a greater understanding of the cycle of birth, life and death or re-birth. If you need help looking into your future taking a few ash leaves to bed and putting them under your pillow will hopefully give you prophetic dreams. There are many healing properties of ash, one being a cure for warts. First you take a clean new pin and prick it into the bark of an ash tree (asking permission first of course) then you prick the wart you wish to be rid of. You can say a little rhyme if you wish at this point, *ash tree, oh ash tree, please take this wart away from me,* is a common one. Then you place the pin back in the tree where you originally pricked it. It's peculiar that witches have frequently been portrayed as warty since there was no need for any of them to tolerate warts if they didn't want to. There is so much mythology connected with ash trees from all traditions that it would definitely require another book to go into them. One very important one we should mention is the story of Odin and the runes from Norse mythology. It is said that in order to gain eternal wisdom he hung himself upside down from ash and received the wisdom of the runes in return for his sacrifice.

The Celts saw it as the tree of re-birth and wands were often fashioned from its wood to use for any magical workings that involved contacting the dead for advice and help regarding the present and future. Because of its water connections it was often seen as the sailor's wood and many lucky talismans were made from it. It is, however, not a tree to be sat under during a thunder storm for like oak it is said to court a flash.

It has similar properties to willow as far as its healing qualities go and decoctions of ash bark are also useful for alleviating rheumatism and other inflammations. The leaves can be infused to produce a laxative but it is very strong (like senna) and should be used sparingly. Children, especially, benefit from exposure to ash and it is a great healer for the young particularly if they are going through illness or great trauma.

HAWTHORN

This gnarled and often-twisted stumpy tree has a lot of love in its heart. It is the tree of the fire festival, Beltane. Growing only up to about thirty feet it can live for up to four hundred years. Traditionally it has always been the favourite hedge tree of farmers. Hawthorn actually means hedge in old English. Its bark is deeply furrowed and it appears old before its time. The leaves are small, five pointed and fairly broad green uppermost and silvery green underneath. It blossoms in May which is where it gets its other name of the maytree. The flowers are either white or pink and very fragrant. The blossom has highly erotic properties and used in balm or massage oil it can have quite startling effects, so watch out – you could get more than you bargained for.

Legends including this tree abound, especially of the Celtic variety, but also more recently too. The Glastonbury thorn, for example, was said to have been brought over here by Joseph of Arimathea in Christ's time. At a later date Cromwell sent a soldier to cut it down but he didn't get very far as he was blinded by one of its thorns. Christ's crown of thorns was supposed to have been hawthorn.

It's main quality is love, however, and most of the legends are love and/or marriage related. To spend time with hawthorn should open your heart and cleanse your soul.

It has amazing fertility properties and can be used in many ways to achieve pregnancy.

Farmers liked the tree as they knew only too well of its healing abilities, especially where cows and horses were concerned. The tree lends itself brilliantly to hedging, being able to re-shoot magically after being sympathetically laid by an experienced hedger. Its powers are magnified if it is found growing next to a well or natural spring.

It will provide help for circulation and heart problems if the leaves are chewed upon or made into a tea sweetened with honey. This will help a sore throat too. It is said that washing in the first dew of the hawthorn on 1 May will cure skin complaints.

Dried hawthorn berries help to cure internal inflammations, e.g. kidney infections and menstrual problems.

It also has a mild sedative effect, so watch you don't overdo it.

The wood traditionally wasn't used a great deal. This was mainly due to the superstitions surrounding the penalties for cutting one down, but a fallen hawthorn could be used and was ok for handles of knives, especially magical ones, and combs or smaller items. Garlands of hawthorn were given at weddings and hung over the marriage bed to ensure a strong and lasting union.

There is another tradition, concerning picking the first hawthorn blossom you see in May and keeping it alive for three days and three nights to draw love to you. This does work but it also has an effect not to be underestimated on the fertility front, so watch-out – you could get two for the price of one.

OAK

This most sacred and mysterious of our native trees is thought of as the king of the forest. Its mighty form once covered large parts of this country. It is very slow growing and can live up to one thousand years old. The trunk is usually short and broad, unless it has to fight for light, in which case it can also grow quite tall. The bark is ridged and furrowed and thick. The leaves are unmistakable and are quite large and long with seven rounded indents. The flowers are to be found as part of a Bach flower remedy which increases your strength and resolve to persevere. The fruit are acorns in the autumn. These can be made into a rather bitter coffee by a process of crushing and distilling twice. It is connected to the summer solstice and the sun. It exudes great love and warmth of a fatherly disposition.

It offers us strength, protection and courage simply by being in its presence for a while. It is also seen as a doorway or portal tree. By meditating near one you can find yourself taken to other realms. Your life battles are often made clearer and easier by its magic as a consequence. It is a great tree to go to when you need to calm down. It forces you to slow down to its speed and helps you to put tensions into perspective. Then its soothing caring side almost puts an arm around you and reassures you that all is well.

The healing properties are astringent and anti-inflammatory but I feel it's a tree best left alone for those purposes. Let us honour it by trying hard to avoid taking any more from this tree. We need to be putting something back where oak is concerned. It wasn't until the Iron Age that oaks were first able to be felled. Then they were decimated thereafter. By medieval times, oaks were being used for such a wide variety of purposes it was hard to find anywhere that didn't have oak about. The shipbuilding and cathedral building accounted for the largest individual cases. The spirit of the oak is still with us but it would be much better if there were a great many more of them about.

That would be a proud inheritance for later generations. The ancient druids met in sacred groves of oaks. Legends and myths abound with famous oaks: King Arthur's story includes Merlin's oak at Carmarthen, Robin Hood's tale includes the Major oak at Sherwood Forest (still alive today) and Herne the Hunter at Windsor park who has no less than three possible contenders, amongst many others far too numerous to mention. Oak trees are not just sacred to our shores – it is the same all over the world wherever they occur.

Carrying acorns is supposed to keep you young in mind body and spirit.

Magically it can be used for any positive purpose. It is also very lucky, being ruled by Jupiter.

HOLLY

The holly king takes over from the oak king in the forest at the winter solstice.

Holly branches are traditionally brought into the house at this time. This is to remind us of the eternal nature of life.

It is evergreen and grows to about thirty to forty feet. It is frequently found with oak trees. It is reluctant to re-locate and rarely survives it. The bark is smooth and ashen/grey/green in appearance. The leaves are thick and shiny with sharp points, except the higher branches which are smooth. The flowers are out in May and the berries start in the autumn and continue for quite a while. The holly is primarily a winter booster. Its contrasting green shiny leaves and red berries gave people a bit of colour through the winter months. It is said that bringing it into the house will harbour the little folk who, grateful to be inside, will do you no harm until 31 January when they must return outside. Putting them back where you found them will help.

Bad luck is thought to pursue anyone who wilfully cuts down a holly tree.

Extreme respect and honour should be in the mind of anyone who takes from the holly.

The berries are extremely poisonous to humans. Superstition has it that if a woman brings smooth holly leaves into the house on solstice eve she will rule the following season; if the husband brings prickly holly in he will rule.

Healing-wise the Bach flower remedy for holly will help people overcome extreme jealousy and harsh feelings towards others. It improves our tolerance and once used you could then follow up with the beech remedy for a while, which does a similar job but mildly.

Magically holly protects and softens our nature. It helps us keep in touch with the wild within on a very positive and creative level.

HAZEL

This prolific native shrub can reach the size of a small tree but rarely gets that far. It is by far one of the most popular trees to coppice and has been for a considerable time. Hazel is commonly found in oak woods and hedgerows. It likes a damp environment. The bark is a smooth beautiful reddish brown and dotted. The leaves are broad, soft and a light green.

The male tree flowers early in the spring and its catkins fill, allowing the pollen to find its way to the female catkins, which are red threads ready for the pollen which they catch and drop down on to the seeds.

The result of their union is the hazelnut.

In the past the hazel played a much bigger part in society than it does now. Its uses were endless. Its elasticity made it perfect for fencing and hurdle making, a skill that is still in demand today in some places. Wattle for housing, smaller carved items such as pipes, basket making, walking sticks, staves, magical wands are all easily crafted from such an obliging wood as hazel.

Mythically hazel has a long association with Celtic Irish tradition. They saw it as the tree of wisdom. It is ruled by Mercury. The wisdom imparted to people from hazel is thought to give you the skill of effective and inspired communication. It has a dreamy quality that asks you to enter its world and use your imagination. Hazel gives you the magical space, a blank canvass and all the imagination you need to fill it. It's a great tree to give you help with expressing yourself and transforming your feelings into words.

It is also known as the poet's tree and inspired Shakespeare, among many others. The faerie realm is thought to be accessible through it. Meditation in a hazel copse can give you a glance at their world if they wish you to see it. The atmosphere around hazel is very enchanted and time can definitely appear to stand still. There must have been a lot of dreamy wattling bards and ovates of old.

Its healing properties were not that prolific. The nuts were seen as a general cure-all and sometimes ground into a paste and mixed with honey for sore throats. Its main healing ability is its feel-good factor. Going to visit hazel when you feel blocked or uninspired will give you the boost you require. It really does lift your spirits.

APPLE

The original native tree from which all later hybrids were formed was the crab apple.

You can still come across wild crab apples. They are quite often seen in our hedgerows and gardens. They rarely grow to any great height but occasionally you can find a really old lady that has made it up to the size of a reasonable tree.

Our modern domestic apples are the result of intensive grafting, and cultivation, of Mediterranean trees in the eighteenth century.

The greenish red leaves are small and shiny heart shapes. It flowers in spring and gives off a wonderful aroma not dissimilar to honeysuckle. The bark is grey and can become quite gnarled with age. The fruit, the apple, appears in the autumn and are small, yellow and hard. They are very bitter and best left to mature a few weeks in a cool dark place before being used.

Apples have a permanent place in history as the fruit of love. Aphrodite, the Greek goddess of love, is strongly linked to them. Gaia's wedding gift to Hera and Zeus was the crab apple. The Celts saw the tree as the original life giving force of humanity, represented by the three drops of life giving energy directly descended from the world of the gods. Burning of an apple tree was considered sacreligious and people would go to great lengths to preserve and protect them. Norse myth accredited crab apple with longevity and would use it to hold back old age.

The healing power of the apple comes into its own when used for the treatment of a broken heart. Grated raw apple is very beneficial as a remedy for morning sickness and funnily enough it's what I instinctively gave my mother when she was pregnant with my brothers. Meditating with apple encourages more trust within and love and respect without. Among the ailments they are believed to cure are diarrhoea, lethargy, high blood pressure, digestive problems and kidney inflammations. Or as the saying goes, 'An apple a day keeps the doctor away'.

It is also one of the most common trees to find mistletoe growing on in the winter.

The wood has somewhat limited uses. It can take a while to stabilize and dry out so it is prone to splitting. It has dense grain and a sweet smell though, and can be very nice to use for smaller items such as handles, love talismans and artistic carvings.

We owe this tree a great deal. All the apples now grown originate from it and we enjoy a huge range of apple-based products as a consequence.

Magically you are most likely to use it for affairs of the heart. If you cut an apple widthways it reveals a five-pointed star. It is said that if you cut one in half this way when you are with your intended and offer them the other half, if they eat it your love is reciprocated.

BLACKTHORN

This spiky little tree or shrub mostly grows in the south of England. It has dark, almost black, smooth bark. It flowers in early spring and is most often found alongside hawthorn, its sister. They are seen as the light and the dark of the seasons. Its fruits are sloes, which are often used in sloe gin and red dye.

It is mostly known for its very long sharp thorns. These can be quite harmful, so huge respect and care needs to be taken when dealing with it. The leaves are quite small and oval in shape.

The thorns are mentioned frequently throughout history and litera-ture. It was believed to be a crown of blackthorn and hawthorn that made up the crown of thorns that Jesus wore on the cross. Witches were often accused of using the thorns to inflict pain and ills upon others. The witch's mark was believed to be caused by a scratch from a thorn.

Sleeping beauty was put to sleep for one hundred years as a result of an encounter with a thorn placed where she would catch it by a dark witch.

At Samhain blackthorn helps us to see through the darkness and offers healing in the winter months. The early spring or Imbolc black-thorn gives us its wonderful blossom and perfume to give us hope and happiness that spring is arrived. The May blackthorn or Beltane, is used as a fertility symbol and for divination or wishes to be granted.

Blackthorn is a brilliant protector, especially psychically. To imagine yourself surrounded by this tree can offer the most effective safety barrier. A wand made from blackthorn will not only offer such protection – it will also be useful for any banishing magic.

It is interesting to note that people who hold on to pain or have much anger inside them seldom get an easy ride from blackthorn and are often the ones who get scratched the worst.

Befriending blackthorn is to invite justice and understanding of what causes negativity into your life. This can be a very interesting and uplifting experience. It certainly makes you think twice before starting any wars – perhaps our world leaders would think twice if they held blackthorn before making war?

The main practical use of blackthorn was and still is hedging.

YEW

Yews are thought to be one of the oldest trees we have. They live to extraordinary ages, some up to 1500 years, and have an unusual way of growing. The branches eventually grow down on to the ground, where they take root, and as the old tree dies so the new one is born. It is not surprising that they are strongly connected with all things eternal, death and birth. The trees themselves can grow to quite a size both in width and height, reaching up to eighty feet. The leaves are thin evergreens and the bark is thick and light to reddish brown with furrows. Its seeds or fruit are little cones.

Older yews are quite often found in churchyards and because of this they seem to have an ecclesiastical connection, which is probably not exclusively justified. They often prove to have been around prior to the churches themselves. It is most likely that the yew was chosen as a good spot to use due to its connections with the dead and the protection it would offer the graveyard. The yew is widely known to be poisonous, another one of its protective properties. The foliage is thick and dark. They flower early but only if in a light position.

Yew was a favoured wood of bowmen and highly sought after for that reason. It has always been seen as unlucky to fell a yew. Due to its strong re-birth qualities it is a useful tree to use in any initiation ceremony. Sprigs of yew can be given to people during attempting contact with departed loved ones.

The yew has no topical applications recommended to it because of its poisonous properties.

ELDER

This common shrub can be found surviving in the poorest of soils and shady positions. It is easy to recognise in late summer due to its prolific berry production. It has sandy coloured bark and grows in a way that makes it looks coppiced but not so. The leaves are medium oval shaped and its flowers a mass of white in late June. They rarely get higher than thirty feet and often grow in clumps. Elderflower cordial and wine are very popular beverages and are still home made by many all over the country.

Mystically it is thought to be the crone spirit and full of ancient wisdom Strangely it is believed by many to bring bad luck if brought into the house. The shoots and subsequent branches are full of soft white pulp, which made it a good choice for whistle making. Elder beads can easily be made this way too; this will of course be tempting fate if you wear them in the house, I presume.

Medically its uses are cooling if applied topically and laxative if ingested. Both the flowers and berries are safe but not the bark. The poor old elder has had a bad name in the past and was once thought to be very evil. This was probably due to the suicidal hanging of Judas Iscariot from one after reporting Jesus to the Romans.

I have found elder a great comfort through difficult times, as have friends of mine. Its a tough old tree with many beneficial uses and reminds us that we must always try to make the best of all situations, not the worst. It certainly encourages positive thinking and slows us down if we are going too fast.

Why hurry?

THE WISE OLD ONES OF NORTH AMERICA

We are not about to venture into the world of the Native American shamanic craft here as this is, as yet, outside my experience and has a bias towards a totemic system, but we can take a brief look at some tree species you can meet in North America. Many of the trees' British relatives have been covered and so in these cases I have avoided duplicating that which has already been said.

GREAT WESTERN RED CEDARS

Although not indigenous they have become one of the northwest's most famous trees. In this environment they grow to the size of giants, only surpassed in size by their cousin the giant sequoia.

Botanically they have flat shiny green leaves and small clusters of cones but the bark is the most memorable. Its red-brown fibrous hull smells amazing and is most popular as an ingredient for incenses. Native Americans would use cedar to cleanse and purify in their smudging rituals. In the right circumstances these trees really do flourish and are spiritually thought to help maintain individuality even when affected by the influences of others. We have several examples nearby in the grounds of an old house and they are truly magnificent against the backdrop of our more humble native trees. They give off a sense of purpose and yet hold great fascination. I feel each one is unique and very pleased to be here. Their element is thought to be fire, which is not at all surprising.

RED ALDER

Not dissimilar to our native alder, the west coast variety has much the same botanical make up with grey bark and broad furry leaves that tend to curl. In the spring it offers its catkins and by autumn the cones have grown that eventually darken through winter and remain attached. It prefers a moist or wet environment but also grows well on ashy soil. It is believed to help one be in the moment rather than looking any farther, and as such it can balance the rational mind with its emotional response. Alder is also great for staying grounded whilst pursuing a dream or goal. It is a harmoniser of the sexes – being bipolar it can always see both sides at once. The moderate temperament of alder is useful for balancing mind and matter. Basically this tree always seems to say, 'It doesn't really matter but it's right sometimes to mind.'

Its healing properties are the same as for our natives above.

WESTERN HEMLOCK

Another giant amongst trees if allowed to grow to fullest potential. They have spruce-like leaves, long and thin, white underneath, and grow either side of their branches. The cones grow from the ends of the twigs, which can flop over with the weight.

It doesn't appear to have any specific healing attributes, unsurprisingly, but does help spiritually in one's ability to ride high waves. Meditating or carrying a sprig of hemlock can help you deal with traumatic circumstances as it relates to difficult times.

For this reason it is a tree of great strength and success in adversity. I haven't any direct experiential contact with this tree so it is only by reading the words of others that we can share in their personal feelings to and from it.

BLACK COTTONWOOD

A broad leaf deciduous tree related to poplars. The leaves are broad based and taper with a leathery finish and wavy ends. Both bear flowers but only the female fruits in summer with capsules that split open. The seeds are not dissimilar to cotton balls hence its name.

Spiritually poplars are unified as their stumps grow back vigorously, making them suitable for coppicing one feels, but also it shows us the resilience of our human body and its capability to regenerate even under supreme tests. It helps us cope with these tests and understand that we should learn to love and accept our physical forms and that rather than trying to escape the body we should all learn to embrace it. This tree sounds marvellous for acceptance and understanding of the need for physical diversity in life and a greater understanding of that which is truly beautiful over that which we generally believe is inflicted on us by society and its perversely consumer based manifestations. True beauty is beneath and the skin is only so deep, says black cottonwood. Accept this and move on.

BIGLEAF MAPLE

This spectacular tree is quite prolific in the Pacific Northwest and has its characteristic wide five-lobed leaves and autumnal helicopter blade seed pods. As with our own maples it is a tree of unconditional generosity of spirit. It encourages us to look beyond our interpersonal relationships and connect with divinity at source through her. This tree offers reassurance that love can be found everywhere and most of all from within oneself, especially when connected with nature. If you have difficulty either giving or receiving love, contact with maple helps you overcome this and dissolves fears of rejection. Its element is air and therefore magically it works through the subconscious, drawing out negativity and transforming it into positive loving thoughts. Not to be confused with the Canadian red maple from which the famous and delicious maple syrup derives, bigleaf maple is slightly different but does have some healing properties. The leaves can be made into an infusion, or eaten in salads surprisingly, but it is best to pick them when very

171

young. This tea is good for pain relief but must be taken frequently for maximum benefit, and also helps to cleanse the liver and spleen. It is high in both calcium and iron, making it an excellent tonic for pregnant women. All of the maple family have something of a practical nature to offer us and the wood is also used for furniture and wand making.

Maple wine can be made by draining sap much in the same way as birch.

COAST LIVE OAK

Although the name conjures up images of groves of oaks just by the sea this species prefers more wooded inland areas. The leaves are in fact evergreen but it does have long narrow acorns making it quite an unusual tree for us here in Britain to conceptualise. The Native Americans would eat the acorns and I presume they heated them first. These trees like the company of their own kind and often form natural groves clustered together. I feel this is a sociable creature but one that discerns and takes its time forming friendships. It encourages us by its nature to slow down a little and enjoy spending quality moments of clear insight without rushing around and never really getting anywhere. If your life is one of high pressure and stress, contact with coast live oak could prove beneficial especially if you have the opportunity to camp near some for a while.

VALLEY OAK

This tall white Californian oak species is the king of the western forests. Much like our indigenous varieties it needs space to really reach maturity but holds on to its regal status unassumingly. The healing and practical usages are also much the same as our native types. Oaks generally have the ability to help us regulate our egos and put them into perspective. As the energy of oak manifests it doesn't seek acknowledgment from elsewhere – it is happy with its own achievements and therefore grows stronger as a result. Great feelings of acceptance and contentment can be experienced through meditating near these great trees. They are also portals to the world of magic, helping both young and old alike connect with the world of fairie.

Doors of opportunity open and oak helps us make the most of each step of our journey and understand true and honest self appreciation.

172

EUCALYPTUS

This semi-evergreen sporadically sheds leaves and is well known to most of us for its essential oil. The tree has pretty blue-green slender leaves and is elegant, often growing tall and slim, rising above it all. It flowers in spring and has a small round seedpod that develops later. It appears to do well in a variety of places and conditions. It isn't indigenous to the country, having been imported from Australia, but is now so prolific that it deserves mentioning. The oil is obtained by crushing the leaves and is great for clearing nasal congestion when burnt in an oil burner. The emphasis from both a healing and magical bias is air and in particular breathing. We often don't breath properly and take shallow breaths rather than deep refreshing ones. The old custom of waking up and opening the window to take a few deep-cleansing breaths in the morning is rarely practised these days, especially by people living in cities – and who can blame them? But if you do have access to fresh air make the most of this natural resource and treat your lungs every day. It improves your oxygen levels and will aid thought and communication.

GIANT SEQUOIA

These magnificent trees have to be the most famous of North America and definitely live the longest. Some are believed to be over three thousand years old, putting our ancient oaks and yews to shame. Thriving in the mountains of Nevada they have become a national emblem for the area. Otherwise known as the sierra redwood, these trees are the ultimate giants, and can measure up to twenty feet in diameter and grow to over two hundred and fifty feet in height. They are evergreens and don't actually begin cone production until they reach sexual maturity at about two hundred years old. They have one of the thickest fire resistant barks in the arboreal world and some may have to withstand many forest fires throughout their lifetimes. They have needles rather than leaves and are most adept at surviving in high altitudes. Sequioas help us see the bigger picture and not to major over minors. They help us understand that all can be overcome and resistance at times is required. They are tough characters that endure and cope well with disastrous situations, helping us to transcend our physical level when required and cope with suffering in a detached way.

They help us realise that by overcoming trauma in life we grow and therefore are closer to spiritual oneness through this experience no matter how hard it may be.

Visiting such trees when going through life-changing transformations or after them can help you come to terms with the pain, suffering and loss you may feel and accept it as part of nature's cycle. Easy to say, I know, but let the love and resilience of the old trees show you how it can be done.

QUAKING ASPEN

Yet another member of the poplar family aspens are unusual though as one tree can become many or many can become one. Their root systems often link up underground connecting each tree with its brothers and sisters. They are broadleafed with round almost heart shaped leaves that flutter noisily in the wind, hence the common name for them. They anchor themselves to the rocky terrain of places such as the Rocky Mountains and are stronger than they look due to their practice of safety in numbers.

They encourage us to place trust in one another and help each other out without a weakening co-dependency. Their ability to help overcome fear is well known, as is their happy buoyant energy. I like to think of them as families of trees all pulling together for a common good but capable of individual free expression outwardly also.

They help manifest ideas and draw the right people together at the right moments, so if you feel alone or in need of a friend visit an aspen and see who else is there!

SHELLBANK HICKORY

Closely related to the shagbank variety of same tree, the shellbank lives in the Allegheny mountains. Once the tree starts bearing its fruit at about forty years old it sheds its bark in strips, renewing itself. There are seven mini-leafs to each individual leaf which are oval in shape and furry underneath. The nuts are popular amongst the squirrel population and are also used for incense and/or included in charcoal production due to their distinctive aroma. The bark is also collected and used for such purposes.

This tree is supposed to help in focusing your energies towards completions of tasks and doesn't encourage short cuts. It encourages attention to details and keeps your mind from straying off track. It is a tree of balance and harmony, specifically of the mind due to it being an air element tree. In a nutshell it naturally triages your priorities and helps you from getting distracted by impulsiveness when it is not required. That is not to say that being impulsive is always bad but there are times to be and times not to be.

RED OAK

This oak tree is a born survivor in many conditions and circumstances. Although its leaves are easily distinguished as oak leaves they have pointed tips more associated with holly. The veins of the leaves are red in colour, hence the name. The acorns are short, round and squat in appearance.

This fiery beastie encourages us to move forward with determination and vigour even if feeling despondent. Following the philosophy of 'that which you seek is here beneath your feet' it says 'the grass is the same all over', so we should not seek escape from situations: rather gain courage to face them head on and make the most of our energy and circumstances. It is a great spiritual energiser and therefore would be worth seeking out if your life has become draining or there is something you feel cowardly about.

SILVER MAPLE

This tree mainly grows in the eastern states of America. It gets its name from the silver underside of its leaves. Although the general shape of the leaves is traditional the lobes are deeper than its friend the sugar maple. The bark flakes as it grows and the seed pods are dual winged.

This tree can be a great healer especially in affairs of the heart as it helps us to focus on the light rather than the shadows of broken love. It can, if allowed, encourage us to move forward from each experience and learn how to give unconditionally. This type of love is normally reserved between parent and child but can manifest into all our relationships if we want it. Much as the wearing of willow leaves or carrying of them after a break up can avoid ill thought or word sent to another, so too can silver maple.

By concentrating on the positive feelings of the past we may possibly draw love to us again but not necessarily from the same direction. By doing this we can heal our own pain and hopefully avoid hurting the lost love left behind.

'Why leave a wake and end up feeling like you are holding one?' says our friend silver maple.

AMERICAN ELM

Our native British elms are sadly few and far between these days after Dutch Elm disease had its fun back in the seventies but some are being reintroduced. In parts of the States the elm is fine and its energy is still readily available for those who come across it. Its multi-trunk grey-ridged bark and unusual asymmetric leaves quite easily distinguish this tree. The leaves are rough to the touch with serrated edges; the seed pods and flowers are visible by May before the tree buds.

This tree is believed to help us connect with our own needs and balance them with the needs of others around us. It says, 'don't sacrifice your own happiness for the sake of another'. If we can't make each other equally happy then elm will help you become aware of this and encourage you to step back from giving selflessly at the cost of your own inner light. Until we understand and acknowledge how much energy and time we can give to another without depleting our own inner light we run the risk of burning ourselves out in a constant effort to please. By putting our own needs first we create our own light and as that strengthens so does empathy and compassion which we can then share with others without really having to do much at all!

SYCAMORE

This highly prolific survivor is a close relative of our own London plane and has the usual massive lobed leaves and mottled bark. Its presence commands attention wherever it grows. The bark flakes off continuously and it has little round ball-shaped seed pods. Given enough room it can grow to quite a height but it prefers to spread out in a magnificent fan shape. It is believed that this tree imbues a sense of individuality and need for self expression even if that means not following the herd. To stand alone in society takes courage but sycamore says, 'Be true to your own heart for that way true happiness lays'. When we attempt to conform we restrict ourselves to the energy patterns of others, which can have its place but not all the time. It wants us to be free to shed our bark and wear our own skin comfortably rather than trying to adopt uniformity.

Sycamore differentiates between necessary conformity, as in mutual positive cooperation in task fulfilment, and individual expression.

So does it really matter if the ambulance guy saving your life has pink hair or a short back and sides? We are measured by our actions not our fashion choices!

And so ends our brief little journey across North America. There are many other species not as yet covered and I for one would like to investigate some of these trees more fully, incorporating some direct experiences. North America has much to offer and I'm sure the spirit of the Green Man is as much a vibrant force in its mountains, valleys, parks and streets as it is here.

SPIRITUAL TREES: A FINAL FEW WORDS

Throughout man's history trees have played an integral part in our evolution on every conceivable level. The knowledge accumulated over this time would in itself present a considerable encyclopaedia. One could dedicate one's whole lifetime to acquiring all there is to know about trees on every level and I'm sure you wouldn't ever finish your journey. We need to open our hearts again to these wonderful beings and let their magic work for us. They really are quite willing if only we are prepared to listen.

Spare a moment for the tree
Stop, still and simply be
Feel that loving energy
Flowing into you for FREE!

DRUIDS

When you ask your average layman their view on druids he or she often refers to the group that descends on Stonehenge each summer solstice or the small group that sat perched on Seahenge trying to protect it from extraction. These people are examples of druids, officially or otherwise.

Druids know in their souls what they are. Nature calls them; her trees and flowers overwhelm them with their beauty and magic. They are drawn to wild and natural places to be at one with their gods and goddesses. It can be described as falling in love with nature. There is of course a lot more to it than that, but it's where it begins. Druids claim their ancestry from the Celts of the past but it is equally possible that a form of Druidry existed before this time. Modern Druidism evolves from an eighteenth century revival.

Most spiritual paths these days express themselves outwardly e.g. Christianity. Druidry is different – it is more of an inward expression. To explain this we should look at the way both paths operate. Christianity encourages us to think of Christ as our saviour and a direct line to a patriarchal God. This it worships in a specific building hallowed for the purpose. It has given us a set doctrine to live within. The emphasis is supposedly on the individual's personal growth but also on their ability to pray and worship and do good deeds, again outwardly.

Druids find spiritual direct contact with nature and know the only saviour we can hope for is ourselves. They go out singularly or in groups to simply be with nature and are enriched spiritually by the experience, so have no need of a specific structure. Druids have no set rules except to take responsibility for yourself and be true to yourself at all times. They often do good deeds but rarely feel the need to shout about it.

It is believed that the Celtic druids would take up to twenty years to achieve any sort of recognition as a local spiritual practitioner. The training was long and hard but the proof is sadly lacking. Songs, stories and poetry were passed down by word of mouth and had to be learnt if you were thought a potential Bard or Ovate supposedly.

This way, it's believed, you acquired the accumulated knowledge, myths and experience of your predecessors. Once this had been achieved you were expected to add to it your own experiential Druidism and in so doing your stories, songs and poetry would add to the rich tapestry. Druid priests also underwent extensive growth spiritually until their masters considered them ready for any sort of initiation rites.

At the heart of Druidism are trees, though. A Druid would be (and still is) expected to get to know each tree on the Ogham. There are thirteen trees on the first path, and guess what – they are the ones listed above.

Each tree would be sat with for long periods and wisdom imparted to those whose hearts were open to receive.

Great insights and healing knowledge was gained by doing this, a practice not dissimilar to the Shamanic path. This is something I strongly advise anyone to do. Each tree has its own strengths and weaknesses, just like us, and is happy to share it with us. By communing with trees on a regular basis you should begin to feel a greater understanding and love for the natural world. Sometimes nature shows you its darker side and this we have to learn to accept as part of the natural cycle of things. This is also part of a Druid's path.

Druids were probably the first group of people who advocated the idea of free speech. Their meetings were held in the open during daylight, giving the impression that nothing was to be hidden. Parliament Hill in London is thought to have been built on the spot of an ancient grove used by Druids and later by the Vikings. The Druids were responsible not only for the spiritual welfare of their tribe or group but also for the conducting of all rites of passage, e.g. marriage, and dealing with judicial matters. They were deeply philosophical people who understood a great deal about the human psyche or condition and had an empathy with people so huge that they were thought of as magical or mysterious. There is magic in Druidry but it seems to be more about an inner knowledge built up over time and their own personal experiences with their gods and goddesses and Dryads or tree spirits.

The name Druid means 'Men of the Oaks'.

Some people are natural Druids and don't realise it. You only have to visit a road protest involving the protection of trees to see that.

Suffice it to say you probably already know if you are drawn down this path or not but even if it's not the path for you it's still invaluable to get a tree connection of some sort into your life.

To find out far more about Druids you can write to the British Druid Order at PO Box 29, St. Leonard's on Sea, East Sussex TN37 7YP or The Order of Bards, Ovates and Druids at PO Box 1333, Lewes, East Sussex BN7 1DX.

7

The Work

This isn't a chapter as such but I wanted to give people a chance to explore their own possible points of interest covered in this book. Listed below are contact names, addresses and web sites that can give you further information on their particular areas of expertise. I've called it The Work as I feel life should really be more about action than words, which is great coming from an author I know, but judge not please.

ENVIRONMENTAL/POLITICAL/SPIRITUAL

British Trust for Conservation Volunteers
36 St. Mary's Street
Wallingford
Oxon OX10 0EU

Friends of the Earth
26–28 Underwood Street
London N1 7JU

Greenpeace
30–31 Islington Green
London N1 8XE

National Trust
36 Queen Anne's Gate
London SW1H 9AS

The Green Party (political arm of the Green movement)
1a Waterloo Rd
London N19 5NJ

or

Green Party
Freepost
Lon 6780
London N19 5BR
www.greenparty.org.uk

http://www.smallwoods.org.uk/links.htm
This is an excellent site for linking up with woodland trusts and related matters all over the UK.

Forestry Commission
Government's official site covering all forestry in UK.
www.forestry.gov.uk

National Trust
A well-established charity that manages huge areas of outstanding beauty including many forests, parks and woodlands.
www.nationaltrust.org.uk/main/policy/documents/ForestWoodlands.pdf

Scottish Woodlands
www.scottishwoodlands.co.uk/management.html

The Real Wood Guide
www.forestsforever.org.uk/realwoodguide5.html

Native Woodland Trust
Forests for Life
www.nativewoodtrust.ie/FFLwwf.html

Woodlands.co.uk
http://woodlands.co.uk/links.htm

The Pagan Federation
BM Box 7097
London WC1N 3XX
http://www.paganfed.demon.co.uk

The official voice of Paganism in UK supporting a huge community that is growing in numbers dramatically each year. Over-eighteen policy, though.

The Green Goddess

Turn and turn about.
Look behind
at the ancient voice of the land.

They came and turned it all about.
Pan into Devil,
Sacred Underworld into Hell,
Creatress into Creator.

Green Goddess into Green Man?

The Green Goddess is also
the power of the Earth.
She, the Giver of Life,
Earth Mother.

Balance is the key.
Female and male together.

Without the Green Goddess
There can be no life.

Without the Green Man
There can be no fertility.

It is their union
that gives to all
the cycles of vegetation,
their gifts of food
and medicine.
Their abundance.
Their creation.

So
Let us open our hearts
to both, and
simply

Put
Her
Back.

Glennie Kindred 12/03

I Heard a voice Say . . .

The forest is the Green Man, all the forests that ever were or will ever be.

This is not just a male energy – it is equally female, as you cannot have one without the other. Nothing in nature is singular.

Men, therefore will do better to work with the Green Lady and women the Green Man. They are part of our own essence and we've always known this.

Love is the key to knowing this energy. You have to be able to love in a generous and unconditional way in order to understand and relate to the energy of nature.

This isn't love the emotion; it's a pure love of creation itself.

My connection was made through a visit by one Hodgoodwind, a faerie elemental who can appear in many forms and is of the air. He told me of this love and I have listened to him ever since.

By thinking of it as an emotion we limit its potential, as it is the force or power that governs the whole universe on this plane and possibly beyond.

As an aspect of the 'one' or God, all knowing, all seeing divine force it appears that the Green Man/Lady operates through love. This is love of all life and all its many forms.

Most of my direct contacts have been through the Goddess, Holda/Holle/Hella and her life giving springs and wells. Although she is often seen as the Queen of the underworld and associated with the season of winter and death this is actually only a process of re-juvenation or re-birth and initiation or evolution, take your pick.

She holds the key to potential new life or a door to tomorrow. Only by returning the running of the planet to nature can we hope for Gaia's or Earth's recovery.

We have to accept our physical limitations and learn to live with them in love.

I feel potentially we have the opportunity to be ultimate creators through access to our inner divinity or becoming the God within.

Self-doubt is often the block to allowing this pure creative force to manifest. So we have become very self-limiting and sadly this is due to a lack of love and confidence in ourselves.

The essence of the Green Man/Lady is the realisation of the creative force that through the necessity of survival resides in all of us. Therefore we must realise our link to the 'whole' of nature and our responsibility to the Green Man/Lady through our actions.

Love.

Part Two
How To Play Conkers!

To play conkers you need to know what a conker is and where to find it in order to then play the game.

Or in other words to meet the Green Man/Lady you must first know what they are and where to find them.

It's a simple analogy that is frequently overcomplicated by our conscious minds.

FFF
Royston Baldock

The Green Man and the Green Lady
By Anna de Benzelle

The images of the Green Man and the Green Lady have been with us from ancient times. They are the personifications of the dual force of nature. They embody the pattern of life, growth, death, decay and new life of the natural cycle – from which most people in Western civilisation have become divorced.

The Green Man and the Green Lady are the impersonal force of nature, given a shape and form that we can relate to. Their green leafy images are most powerful and speak to our deep unconscious – a prod to remind us of our place in the natural world. But they appear in other guises with a slightly altered emphasis – for example there is the Nut Brown Maid who puts in fleeting appearances in some of the ancient ballads and the Queen of Elphame, the Green Lady wearing other clothes. There are the stories of Puck or Robin Goodfellow, the spirit of the greenwoods, who is clearly the Green Man under another name.

A simplified way of expressing the force that the Green Man presents is to use the image of a seed – an acorn for example. Locked up in this small seed is the huge potential of the full grown oak tree, the notion of a great span of time – the life of an oak tree can be very long indeed – and the potential that the tree itself has. It will produce vast quantities of new acorns every year once it is a mature tree and eventually may provide the wood to build or make something that will last for yet more years. This driving force of potential creation which is contained within a seed is a synonym for the Green Man. Such he is – a constant driving force of life.

The Green Lady, however, has to do something with this creative force, so her emblem is the cup – possibly even the cup that the acorn sits in. She makes the form that contains the energy of the Green Man and gives it shape. Without her there would be nothing but a roaring force, unconfined, shapeless and useless. With the creation of form comes the containment of the life force and therefore limitation and death, as it eventually transmutes and changes.

The cup of form can be seen as an earthen cup, made of clay; a crystal cup made of stone that forms the skeleton of our planet or even as the bowl-shaped rocks, worn away with the constant pounding of water at the very bottom of a waterfall – another form of the life force of the planet, caught and shaped and channelled.

186

The Green Man and the Green Lady are the two joint forces of life working in the rocks, the earth, the sky, the sea and in every plant, animal and human being. The Green Man and the Green Lady are all of us. We need to give them expression and honour. They contain the perfect balance of all creation.

A Message from the Green Man
From *The Silver Branch Cards*, by Nicholas R. Mann 2001

Given that the earth does not belong to you, but that you belong to the ceaseless flow of life on earth, and given that you do not belong to your body, but that your body belongs to your soul, then the conclusion from these two truths is that the life of the earth and the life of your soul are one and the same.

Given the common perception that the flow of life on earth is in peril – that species are being destroyed and human actions will lead to the collapse of the systems that support life – then the inescapable conclusion from this is that there is perception of a threat to the existence of your soul.

It is unnecessary to speak about the future of life and the earth. Life and the earth will continue. The question is over the future of the incarnations of your soul in the stream of life the earth now offers. If the purpose of incarnation is to learn wisdom from all possible existences, the loss of this stream means that the opportunities for learning this wisdom are disappearing. Your soul will incarnate without the possibility of learning what the existence has to offer. It is as though life for the soul on earth is becoming numb. Your soul incarnates to learn in the world of nature more of the steps of the dance that it does with its lover in the infinite. This world, this life, has always offered exceptional opportunities for this. This world is not greater nor is it any lesser than any other experience in the universe – indeed, this beautiful world perfectly mirrors the universal dance of love – it simply presents it in its unique terms.

If you live outside of the steps of the pattern offered by nature – if you cannot see, touch, smell or hear the qualities of the elements provided by the natural cycles of life – then your incarnations will no longer experience the fullness of the universal dance that nourishes the soul. You will increasingly live in an artificial world created by technology. Such artificial worlds are attractive to your incarnations. They are glamorous and seductive, and they appeal to the needs of the body, but no care or love is held within them. There is no growth in them, only entropy. There is no ebb and flow in them, no diffusion and concentration of elemental power, there is none of the breath of the universal dance.

The soul cannot expand into the world and discover itself and its beloved in the soul of nature when the environment is composed of elements that have destroyed life to come into existence. You know what I am describing: concrete, plastics, synthetic compounds. However much the mind and body may be attracted to them, the soul shudders and turns away from food that has no sustenance, from matter and energy that does not add to the life of the whole. Much of what now sustains you has destroyed more life than it has created.

There is a sense of this impending situation, and artists are depicting it in their work. Films and books describe scenes where nature has vanished. Nuclear accidents, massive pollution, radiation, earthquakes and meteor strikes pound the planet. There is an obsession with sealed or underground shelters, with space-stations and other artificial environments created as substitutes for the natural environment of the earth. Yet you know there is no substitute. Your incarnations might survive for a time in such environments, but not live, learn, love and become wise in them.

In the desire to hold on to what is felt to be slipping away, pressure will be placed upon the few natural places that remain on earth. In the search for soul, the ability of my vast plains, deserts, oceans, forests, mountains and rivers to sustain life will become limited.

Technologies that destroy life will come into the hands of those who do not understand the nature of their longing for it. They – perhaps scientists, generals, politicians, religious zealots or the developers of the materialist culture – will have the ability to strike down huge portions of life at any moment. Under these circumstances, your incarnation will find it hard to learn the steps of the dance with spirit. In places, wars will be conducted as tides of fear, rage, irrationality, envy and hatred created by the sense of the loss of soul race through the people. The ideas, religions, ideologies and beliefs generated by the dominant cultures will devour all, as those who are enslaved by them seek to satisfy the loss and emptiness felt within.

Remember, the life of the earth is the life of the soul. This life depends upon rich and healthy relationships between all of its parts. True wealth is measured in love and care, not in power or possession. Wealth is measured in the quality of the micro-organisms you are host to. Wealth is measured by the quality of air in your lungs, the images before your eyes, the sounds in your ears, the music in your mind, the blood pulsing in your veins, the water in the rivers, the love you have for all life.

Free the mind from distraction. Empty the mind of belief. Empty the mind of any condition that is not grounded in life. Allow common sense, earth-wisdom and power to come welling up from within. Trust that the natural qualities of gratitude, prayerfulness, kindness, wonder, love, compassion, generosity, imagination, curiosity, caution, discernment, creativity and intelligence will be within you whenever you need them. Know they are present in others.

See the life of nature as sacred. See every tree and stone, insect and leaf, water droplet and wind, charged with the immanent presence of the divine. See the soul in every landscape; in every being and in every word they speak. Life, the soul of nature and the universe, is always willing to reveal itself to you in new forms. Learn how to dance with life as though it were your lover! Do not try to hold onto any part of it.

Every act of love is a step of the dance with the infinite. Bring the whole self into love. Learn to sing, to dance, to praise, to give birth and to give thanks to the tides of the universe moving through life.

Be all that it is possible to be in words of love, words of life, words that flow outward from the soul. Be the best that you can be. See the wonder in every living thing. And when all is done, and life no longer spirals up within the body, lie down on the forest floor, knowing that the words of the song continue in the dance of pure energy that moves throughout the universe.

Suggested Further Reading

Reclaiming the Gods (Magic, Sex, Death & Football)
Nicholas Mann
Green Magic, 2002
ISBN 0-9536-6318-3

Organic Gardening
Pauline Pears & Sue Stickland
R.H.S
Mitchell Beazley, 1995

The Woodland Way
Ben Law
Permanent Publications
ISBN 1-8562-3009-0

Portrait of Epping Forest
Sir William Addison
Hale
ISBN 0-7091-6130-1

Meetings with Remarkable Trees
Thomas Pakenham
Weidenfeld & Nicolson
ISBN 0-297-83255-7

The Attentive Heart
Conversations with Trees
Stephanie Kaza
Fawcett Columbine

Epping Forest Then and Now
Winston G. Ramsey and Reginald L. Fowkes
Battle of Britain Prints International Ltd.
ISBN 0-900913-39-8

The Celestine Prophecy
James Redfield
Bantam Books
ISBN 0-553-40902-6

Our Origin and Destiny: An Evolutionary Perspective on the New Millennium
Kathy L. Callahan
A.R.E. Press
ISBN 0-87604368-6

The Green Consumer Guide
John Elkington and Julia Hales
Gollancz
ISBN 0-575-04177-3

Mysterious Stranger
David Blaine
4 Books
ISBN 0-7522-1989-8
(and any subsequent publications)

Flower Poems
John Clare
Edited by Simon Kovesi
Oxford Brookes University
ISBN 974-87960-9-4

Bibliography

Tree Wisdom
Jacqueline Memory Paterson
Thorsons
ISBN 0-7225-3408-6

The Sacred Tree
Glennie Kindred
ISBN 0-9532-2275-6

Tree Ogham
Glennie Kindred
ISBN 0-9532-2272-1

The Quest for The Green Man
John Matthews
Gosfield
ISBN 1-84181-1111-4

Pan: Great God of Nature
Leo Vinci
Neptune Press
ISBN 0-9505-0018-6

Green Man: The Archetype of Our Oneness with the Earth
William Anderson
Compass
ISBN 0-9517-0381-1

The Wildwood King
Philip Kane
Cappall Bann
ISBN 1-8983-0768-7

The Green Man: Companion and Gazetteer
Ronald Miller
S.B. Publications
ISBN 1-8577-0131-3

The Green Man: A Field Guide
Clive Hicks
Compass
ISBN 0-9517-0382-X

Tree Medicine, Tree Magic
Ellen Evert Hopman
Phoenix
ISBN 0-9193-4555-7

Green Magic
Lesley Gordon
Ebury Press
ISBN 0-8522-3117-2

The Green Man: Tales from the Mythic Forest
Edited by Ellen Datlow and Terri Windling
Viking
ISBN 0-6700-3526-2

Trees for Healing
Pamela Louise Chase and Jonathon Pawlik
Newcastle Publishing Co. Inc.
ISBN 0-8787-7157-3

In Search of Herne the Hunter
Eric L. Fitch
Cappall Bann
ISBN 1-8983-0723-7

Hedgewitch by Rae Beth
Robert Hale Limited, 1990

The Little Book of the Green Man
Mike Harding
Aurum Press Limited 1998
(and any subsequent publications!)

Bibliography

A Practical Guide to the Runes
Lisa Peschel
Lleweylln Publications, 1999

Gods, Demons and Symbols of Ancient Mesopotamia
Jeremy Black & Anthony Green
British Museum Press, 1992

DARK MOON DESIGNS

Dark Moon Designs are taken from the original paintings of Jane Brideson and inspired by the cycle of the seasons, the moon and our sacred earth.

Our range of full colour cards and prints includes the eight festivals of the Wheel of the Year, Celtic Goddesses and Gods, Green Men, Lunar Cycle and many more.

For a full colour catalogue please send a cheque/postal order for £4.00 or $6.00 made payable to DARK MOON DESIGNS to the address below. Alternatively you can visit our website at: www.darkmoondesigns.net

Dark Moon Designs,
Rainbow Cottage,
Clonduff,
Rosenallis,
Co. Laois
Republic of Ireland
Email: morrigan@mac.com